T0341531

DESIGNERS OF THE FUTURE

WHO SHOULD MAKE THE DECISIONS?

D. GARETH JONES

MONARCH
BOOKS

Oxford, UK & Grand Rapids, Michigan

Published by Monarch Books
an imprint of
Lion Hudson plc
Wilkinson House, Jordan Hill Road,
Oxford OX2 8DR, England
Email: monarch@lionhudson.com
www.lionhudson.com/monarch

ISBN: 978-1-85424-708-7

First edition 2005

Acknowledgments
Unless otherwise stated, Scripture quotations are
taken from the Holy Bible, New Revised Standard Version,
© 1973, 1978, 1984 by the International Bible Society.
Used by permission of Hodder and Stoughton Ltd.
All rights reserved.

A catalogue record for this book is available
from the British Library.

Contents

Preface

For some, reference to designers in the title of this book will immediately raise the spectre of unease. But why? Designers pose no problems when what we have in mind is furniture or clothes or bridges. No one in their right mind would ever object to the notion that objects like these have to be designed. Not only this, but part of their cost lies in the design element. We pay for good design. But when we turn to human beings, the very thought that other humans may have some part to play in their design is anathema to many. The last thing we want is for our children, let alone ourselves, to be the result of human design. That is to be left to God, or nature, or genetics; take your pick as long as there is no human interference. This is the one place where we are not to intrude, and it is decidedly the one place where human design is off-limits.

Who makes the decisions? There is no doubt that biomedical scientists are intimately involved. We can view them and their activities as a source of blessing and hope, or we can opt for the complete opposite, that is, they are a source of strife and despair. Here we have the antitheses – heaven or hell, welcome them into our midst or cast them out as wretched interlopers. Of course, as is nearly always the case, the truth lies somewhere between these extremes; they are neither saints nor sinners, but some mixture of the two. And yet, this middle way can be difficult to find when confronted by such notoriously emotive topics as cloning or stem cell research or genetic engineering. All too readily we reach for labels that bring productive discussion to a rapid end: we are playing God or designing babies or killing embryos.

My fervent hope is that I can wend my way through this morass of highly emotional but also unnervingly challenging areas. I do so from a Christian perspective, but as a Christian who is well aware of the tentative nature of so much of what I write. And I write as a biomedical scientist, an admission that alone may consign me in the eyes of some to the "dark side". Even before I write a single word, my bias is showing through. After all, I won't be automatically condemning all that bio-medical scientists do (I have earned my living as one for many years!). Nevertheless, neither shall I be worshipping at any biomedical altar. I am close enough to the science as well as to many practitioners of the science to be well aware of the numerous pitfalls of the scientific endeavour. But, by the same token, I am also well aware of the myriad contributions it can make to our lives together as human beings.

And so while I may have lived for many years on the "dark side", I also contend that I have always had a foot in the "light side". This emanates from my Christian commitment that has constantly brought me back to recognition of our dependence upon God the Father as creator and sustainer of the universe, Jesus Christ as Lord and Saviour of mankind, and the Holy Spirit as encourager and upholder of the people of God. It is my hope that some of the values that stem from this commit-ment will emerge in the pages that follow, especially perhaps values such as humility, the centrality of serving others and living for others, and the importance of nurturing the rela-tionships we have as humans living in communities.

While the topics dealt with here follow on from those I

have dealt with in books such as *Valuing People: Human Value in a World of Medical Technology,* and *Clones: The Clowns of Technology?,* the pace of scientific developments has necessitated a re-examination of what I wrote just a few years ago both to bring it up-to-date and also to reassess it. This does not mean I have made substantial changes to stances I held in the 1990s, but a fair degree of nuancing has inevitably taken place.

My emphasis is a focused one – mainly at the beginning of human life and development, and genetics and neuroscience. These reflect my own areas of interest and expertise, but they also touch on pressure points in contemporary medicine. This is where many exciting scientific developments are taking place, developments that appear to be challenging traditional perceptions of what it means to be human. In other words, the speed of scientific advance is not merely of interest for its own sake; these scientific revolutions bring in their wake ethical, social and theological revolutions. Or that at least is how it seems.

There is no getting away from the ever-increasing power of biotechnology, especially medical technology. For some commentators, the replacement of organs, the use of stem cells to repair tissues, the desire for healthier children, the human genome project, and attempts at increasing the lifespan, are all illustrations of hubris. They are as readily associated with illicit enhancement and eugenics, as they are with legitimate therapy. These concerns are elaborated in *Beyond Therapy: Biotechnology and the Pursuit of Happiness,* the report of the President's Council on Bioethics in the United States. Underlying this report is the power of what it sees as our limitless desire to be more than human.

In tackling issues like these I have become acutely aware of the gulf between where much scientific thought and interest is at, and where theological exploration is concentrated. While it would be misleading to make grand generalisations, there is little doubt that popular Christian thought and popular scientific thought are poles apart. Is this because Christian and scientific thought do indeed reside on different continents, or is it because at least some Christian understanding of prevailing science is inadequate? It is my belief that the latter is the case, and this book is presented as a contribution in this area.

In a book like this one I am inevitably crossing disciplinary boundaries, and this is always a dangerous venture. I am a scientist who is delving into theology and into ethics; I am a neuroscientist who is dealing with genetics and developmental biology. And I am a Christian who sees virtue in scientific ventures. But I have no choice if I am to bring together in the one person (myself) all these diverse and sometimes apparently contradictory contributors to an understanding of the very earliest stages of human existence. Whether I like it or not, I am walking a tightrope, but if I am to be faithful to the different facets of my calling, I have no option. A tightrope it is, and I hope that you will walk it with me.

This book is an expansion of a series of four lectures I delivered at Liverpool Hope University College in April 2004, during a period of research and study leave. The opportunity to present these lectures was very graciously provided by Professor Gerald Pillay, the Rector, and they were delivered under the auspices of the Humanities Deanery. I am most grateful for this opportunity and for the hospitality so generously provided by the College and by Professor Kenneth Newport in Theology and Religious Studies. It was indeed a pleasure and gave me an opportunity to explore further issues that I have been writing about over the past few years. The chapters on the human embryo and stem cells are adaptations of articles written during the same period of leave, when I was a Visiting Fellow at St Edmund's College, Cambridge. This Fellowship was made possible by Sir Brian Heap, Master of the College, and was facilitated in many ways by Dr Denis Alexander, a Fellow of the College.

I would like to thank the University of Otago for providing me with this period of research and study leave in the first half of 2004, a very rich period of thinking and writing in the midst of what is normally a life filled with a host of administrative and teaching duties. It was also a pleasure to spend so much of it quietly with my wife in the idyllic and highly civilised surroundings of Cambridge.

I am also grateful to Dr Kerry Galvin for her assistance with literature searches, subediting, and checking all facets of the finished product.

Many thanks to Alicia Geddes and Maja Whitaker for their assistance at the page proof stage.

Gareth Jones
Dunedin

Chapter 1

Should We be Meddling in God's World?

How often have we heard the expression "playing God"? It seems to have become synonymous with many facets of modern science. And yet, while it is applied in numerous different contexts, the predominant one to which it is linked is that of modern medicine and present-day biomedical research. It seems to be confined to activities that involve direct scientific control over human beings, especially at the beginning and end of our existence. Investigations into astronomy don't appear to elicit this condemnation – and activities regarded as akin to playing God generally do evoke condemnation – perhaps because they give the impression of being confined to describing, with ever-increasing precision and sophistication, what happens a long way away from us, or events that occurred an unbelievably long time in the past. These things happened, and all these particular scientists are trying to do is fathom their mysteries. The same can be said of chemists or geologists or botanists. All these are unravelling the secrets of nature, even if some groups may be unhappy with the interpretations or hypotheses with which these scientists sometimes emerge.

Even architects and engineers, who design and build startlingly imaginative and unusual buildings or bridges, don't appear to be playing God. They may be criticised on aesthetic grounds; their designs may not be appreciated; but they aren't usually condemned because they have taken on themselves the mantle of God, by erecting vast skyscrapers or buildings that seem to defy the laws of gravity. These designers are demonstrating enormous creativity, and yet their creativity is not seen to be treading on the toes of a creative God.

But once biomedical scientists enter the picture, all this changes. Curing diseases, life-saving surgery and finding remedies for the common cold or AIDS are acceptable, even though some of these activities have far-reaching implications for individuals and society. These do not generally acquire the opprobrium of going too far and playing God. But tinkering with the genome, interfering with reproduction and modifying embryos are all examples of playing God. They touch a very sensitive nerve, and they elicit the deepest of concerns. In some manner they are seen as intruding into what we are, into the very essence of our being, so that we will end up different from what we are now. The very course of human life might be changed, and by definition the change will be for the worse. And so it is important to ask whether we should be meddling at all in God's world, or at least in this particular part of his world.

Are we playing God?

Consider the following illustrations from the reproductive sphere:

Illustration 1

Geoff and Cindy have a baby by perfectly natural means. They are both reasonably fertile and have no difficulty in conceiving. Everything is straightforward, and medical technology enters the picture only in very peripheral ways. In bringing a new human being into the world, are Geoff and Cindy playing

God? After all, they have done something quite stupendous, since someone who didn't exist now does exist. This is probably the most creative act in which they will ever take part. Let's take this a little further, and say that Geoff and Cindy have been married for five years, but only now have they decided to have a baby. It's fair to assume they could have had one four years ago, but they decided not to. Were they playing God in putting off childbearing for four years?

Illustration 2

Luke and Carrie have been unable to have a baby quite as easily, but have now succeeded with the assistance of *in vitro* fertilisation (IVF). Fertilisation was carried out in the laboratory using Luke's sperm and Carrie's eggs. Eight embryos were produced and two were implanted in Carrie's uterus; these resulted in a single child. The remaining six embryos were frozen for future use by the couple. An artificial element has been introduced into the process, by means of which their subfertility has been bypassed. In this instance, the creativity has been brought about with human assistance. Is this going too far? Is it playing God in a questionable manner?

Illustration 3

Graeme and Amanda have also just had a child by IVF, but in this case there were probably no fertility problems. Amanda was a ballerina and decided she wanted to have as long a career as possible before having children. And so, when they were in their mid-20s, they underwent IVF and nine embryos were produced. These were frozen to be used later at a convenient time. The couple decided this time had come when Amanda turned 39. She intends having another child in two years' time. Are Graeme and Amanda playing God? They have resorted to IVF for social reasons, and have deliberately postponed having a family until relatively late in the normal reproductive period. Of course, they could have done this without using IVF, although their chances of conceiving would probably have been much lower.

Illustration 4

Greg and Bronwyn have heard of pre-implantation genetic diagnosis (PGD), which will enable them to have a child of whichever sex they want. It is an expensive procedure, and they will have to use IVF. But they have decided they want a boy, and that is what they get. In this instance, they have over-ridden the usual factors that result in what normally seems like a lottery. They would like their next child to be a girl, and they are assured that can be arranged. Are they playing God? Some people would describe the resulting child as a "designer baby", since deliberate efforts have been made to get a particular sort of child for purely social reasons. Can this be justified?

Illustration 5

Mike and Sally have just had a child by IVF, but what is unusual about this birth is that Sally is 60. She has had a high-powered career, and until recently had shown no interest in children. She certainly didn't want one to interfere with her career aspirations, especially since it was obvious she wouldn't make it to the highest echelons of her profession alongside the demands of a baby and growing child. The birth was made possible by using an embryo donated by another couple, and treating her appropriately, since she is obviously post-menopausal. In giving birth to a child at this advanced age, numerous biological obstacles have had to be overcome. Are Mike and Sally doing something objectionable?

Illustration 6

Paul and Simone have tried unsuccessfully to have a baby for ten years. This has included three years of IVF-assisted attempts. However, Simone's sister agreed to act as a surrogate, and has successfully carried Paul and Simone's embryo to term. A baby has been born, and Paul and Simone are delighted. They have a baby at last. But have they played God? Another individual has been involved in the whole process, and so they have moved even further from a standard form of reproduction. Have they moved into what should be forbidden territory?

These illustrations could be repeated countless times in this and many other areas. There would have been no difficulty in providing more extreme examples, but these will suffice. In each case, the couples have made decisions that have influenced their childbearing. In each case, a child has finally been born. But have these couples taken on the mantle of God, doing what should be left to him? Is any intervention in the reproductive process an intervention too far? Should we disapprove for theological reasons, because we may be usurping God's role as creator?

Is there anything wrong with playing God?

The notion of playing God raises its head in most scientific domains, the intended message being that this is *forbidden territory*. The term is generally used negatively; it is usually a term of abuse. We are going where we should not be going. We are walking into an area that should be left to God. It is as though we are out on a walk, and ahead of us lies a field surrounded by a fence and a gate. There is no notice on the gate forbidding us from entering, but we assume that the fence by itself is enough to warn us that this is not somewhere we should wander. We should walk around the field or turn back. The field is God's field and we are mere human beings.

Not only this, but the word "play" signifies a meddling with serious matters (Dutney, 2001). We do not have to play, and we do not have to indulge in these activities. Not only are we entering forbidden territory, we are doing so *needlessly*. Life would be much safer if we left well alone, if we did not play with fire. Why do we not accept that we are limited beings and that there are certain things outside our grasp?

"Playing God" generally has connotations of going where we should not be going; enquiring into things that should lie outside the scope of our interests. It is going too far, and is treading on the toes of God. We are aiming to become Godlike in our powers (Peters, 2003a). In theological terms, it is often seen as our eating from the tree of good and evil, succumbing to the temptation to be like God, and refusing to accept God-ordained limitations. The diffuse nature of the phrase is, of course, a hindrance and can cause considerable confusion. Also, different people may well be employing it in different ways. Occasionally, it is seen as deliberately setting out to replace God with something human, as a form of overt idolatry. However, I am not convinced that this is its usual sense.

Peters (2003a) considers that "playing God", what he calls an "enigmatic phrase", can have three overlapping meanings. It is learning God's awesome secrets, a benign meaning. Or it can refer to the wielding of power over life and death, a meaning that strangely seems to be confined to medical doctors. It is with this meaning that we encounter the notion of an overstretching of human abilities, with human beings intruding into realms that rightfully belong to God and doing so on account of their hubris or pride. A third meaning takes this second one further, and focuses on scientists as they seek to alter life and influence human evolution. It is with this meaning that humans are condemned for substituting themselves for God whenever they seek to determine how some elements of human nature might be directed in the future. It is in this context that fears galore centre on altering human genes, and on intruding into the sacred core of what we are as human beings.

All too readily, the fears underlying human abilities in genetics in particular assume theological overtones, leading to the emergence of what can be interpreted as a new divine commandment: "You shall not play God". Translated into biomedical terms, this generally means: "You shall not interfere with the human genome; you shall not touch human DNA; you shall not conduct research on human embryos." No matter what positions we emerge with on these specific issues, it is crucial to remember that not one of these entities is either sacred or ultimate. God alone is sacred; God alone is ultimate; all that God has made is good; on the other hand, nothing that God has made is itself god. Hence, by definition, no technological intervention can violate God's rule; to think that it can is to worship nature and not the creator (Bouma *et al.*, 1989).

For me, the notion of "playing God" is not nearly as negative and oppressive as it is frequently considered. The criticism that a procedure is akin to "playing God" tends to reflect hostility towards the procedure rather than presenting a clear rationale as to the manner in which it transgresses divine boundaries. Many years ago, the theologian Paul Ramsey commented that human beings should not play God before they have learned to be human beings, and when they are human beings they will not want to play God (Ramsey, 1970). While this makes a superb quotation, it fails to throw any light on what human beings should or should not do in any scientific area. The most one tends to elicit from such uses of the term is that the present human form is divinely ordained and should not be modified in any manner, leaving in limbo the numerous uses made of vaccines, antibiotics, surgery, preventive medicine and genetic counselling. Are these illustrations of "playing God" in the sense that they should not have been undertaken? Or do we recognise their value and their contribution to the well-being of people and whole populations? Even if we do recognise their positive side, was this accepted in the early stages of their development, before they had proved themselves useful? In other words, it is far easier to make a retrospective assessment than a prospective one.

From a Christian standpoint we are made in God's image, and hence are to function like God. No matter how much our Godlikeness has been shattered by sin and rebellion against God, we are still images of our maker, even if tarnished ones (Genesis 1:26–27; 5:1; 1 Corinthians 11:7; Colossians 3:10; James 3:9). Consequently, we demonstrate a great deal of his creativity and his inquisitiveness. Humans as scientists are humans as God's images, probing and thrusting into the creation, attempting to understand it and redirect it as God's stewards (Jones, 1987; Peterson, 2001). Within the medical sphere, the desire is to exercise at least limited control over evil in the form of diseases that would otherwise ravish and destroy all that is beautiful and worthy in God's world. Underlying all such attributes is a proviso, namely, that the control is exercised in a responsible manner (Genesis 1:26, 28; 2:19; Psalm 8:6–8).

When this is not the case, we see the other side of the picture: the arrogance of scientists. This, of course, is certainly not universal, any more than all politicians are motivated by nothing other than power or business people are always driven solely by profit. And yet it has to be acknowledged that some scientists on some occasions may be arrogant and unworthy, with motives of self-aggrandisement and personal glory. They may show little regard for the welfare of individual humans, even when the realm within which they are working is that of medicine. We have to agree that any attempt to create some new humanlike creature with superlative powers would stem from human conceit and the notion that human abilities are unlimited. However, this is hardly the stuff of everyday science, and anyone who even contemplated such a venture would be "playing the devil", rather than playing God.

From a Christian perspective, we are not to use massive scientific powers for superficial and frivolous ends (Jones, 1999). There are always dangers, and to risk these for minor gains is dangerous and irresponsible. Much of the criticism of genetics revolves around its possible insubstantial uses, such as gene manipulation for eye colour or facial features. Such criticism is justified, but this is criticism of the *misuse* of genetics rather than of genetic advance itself. Similar criticism can be made of the misuse of many other technological developments, and even of human abilities themselves. Humans playing God only become dangerous when they fail to utilise their Godlike capabilities in ways that will deepen and enrich the lives of other human beings.

These negative images have to be taken seriously, and yet they fail to negate the overall thrust of much scientific advance. Genetic advance per se is not synonymous with pride and arrogance, any more than advances in immunology or keyhole surgery are illustrations of pride and arrogance. Genetic advance is not an aping of God's power, since all forms of genetic therapy owe their rationale to his power. As long as the aim of genetic therapy is the alleviation of human illness, it has the potential to elevate human beings as God's images. Nevertheless, there are always dangers, and the notion of "playing God" should remind us that we are only to modify fundamental biological processes with enormous caution and deep humility. There is much we do not know, and there is much over which our control is tenuous and fragile at best. At its highest level, playing God is an exercise in responsibility, demanding intelligence, compassion and spiritual discernment. It is not an exercise to be entered into frivolously.

Ordinary people playing God

But *who* is playing God? The general assumption is that it is doctors and scientists. These are the groups within society who are tempted to transgress boundaries. This is interesting, because we don't generally seem to think that artists or composers "play God" in this negative sense. Did Picasso play God, or Henry Moore, or Jackson Pollock? Probably not. What then about Bach, or Mahler, or John Tavener? We would probably be more inclined to say that some at least of these glorify God in their compositions; in no way are they usurping his authority. Why, then, do we tend to set apart the activities of scientists?

But this question of *who* is playing God goes even further than this. Think of those earlier reproductive scenarios. The couples were the decision-makers. And so, if anyone is playing God, it's them, it's *us*, it's ordinary people, and not arrogant scientists. Let's take this further with another illustration.

Think of a couple with cystic fibrosis in the family. In their first pregnancy some years ago they had reason to be concerned that the fetus might have cystic fibrosis (Jones, 1999). Via amniocentesis, some fetal cells were tested using a gene probe for cystic fibrosis. They knew beforehand that, if this turned out to be positive, they would have a choice to make – either continue with the pregnancy knowing that the child would be afflicted with this debilitating and distressing condition, or have an abortion.

These two young people had to make agonising choices. These are ordinary people, without any sophisticated scientific or theological knowledge, having to determine the fate of embryos and children who will one day become adults. The situation facing them is not of their own making; they would never have elected to have to cope with a tragic disease like cystic fibrosis. They have no control over the gene underlying this condition. The decisions they make have nothing to do with heroics or hubris. They are trying to sort out the dimensions of their family life in the midst of burdens and tears.

If we continue to use this term "playing God", we can say that they are forced to play God, not because of arrogance but because of necessity. They have to act responsibly, by choosing what they hope will be the better path, even though they are pitifully aware of the morally tainted nature of *any* choice they make. Whatever they do, momentous decisions are being taken. To employ the language of playing God, these people have to play God because they *must* play God. It is their responsibility to make decisions, and these decisions involve the fate of human beings. In a far less dramatic situation one can say that whenever a couple decide on when to have or not to have children, the same principle applies. Similarly, the decision to agree to the undertaking of a delicate and far from predictable operation on a child is a momentous one and falls into the category of playing God, albeit with the very best of intentions.

Let us now imagine that, a few years further on, the couple with cystic fibrosis in their family wish to conceive again. On this occasion they are informed that the embryo itself can be genetically tested before it has a chance to implant in the uterus. This is the technique of pre-implantation genetic diagnosis (PGD), for which two cells will be removed from an early embryo (see Chapter 2). If PGD shows that the embryo does not have any indication of cystic fibrosis, it will be transferred to the woman's uterus in the normal way. On the other hand, if the tests are positive, the embryo will be discarded and the same procedure will be carried out on a second embryo. This will be repeated until a negative result is obtained.

The couple are now confronted by a different set of dilemmas, revolving around the respective values of a four- or eight-cell embryo and a child. Once again, they can be said to be playing God by making decisions with profound implications for at least one future individual, and even for those who will never develop beyond being very early embryos. It is their family and their children that are at stake, and this couple are making truly godlike decisions. They have no choice, since for them there is no escape from the reality of cystic fibrosis and its devastating effects on any children they bring into existence. In a futuristic scenario, one can envisage the use of gene therapy to modify embryos, thus bringing us into the area of genetic manipulation.

What should have emerged here is that the transition from conventional approaches to genetic ones has been gradual. We have moved into high technology, and yet the decision-making is not dramatically different from that of a less sophisticated era. This form of technology has not suddenly introduced the notion of playing God. That has been present all along; only its dimensions have changed.

There will be risks, and people like the young couple will have to exercise responsibility. But this is what being human is all about. We cannot claim that we are made in the image of God, and then walk away from what that means – exercising responsibility, attempting to improve the world for ourselves and others, understanding as much as we can, and controlling what can be controlled. Playing God like this is essential for Godlike creatures. No matter how dangerous this sounds, it protects us from the illusion that we actually are gods and that we can do anything. As we play God, we should realise that we have limitations, and that ultimately we are utterly dependent upon the one who is our creator.

I have retained this term "playing God" for the sake of simplicity, in order to draw a contrast between its negative connotations and what I take to be far more positive ones. It may not be the best term from a Christian angle, but it has the merit of immediacy. It has the connotations of fulfilling a God-given mandate to serve others, to care for the vulnerable, and to heal. It acknowledges that humans are to participate in the process of transforming the world, by sustaining, restoring and improving what has been temporarily entrusted to us. The material world (including human beings) could be better than it is, and humans have the responsibility to attempt to achieve this, albeit in a limited fashion. While pride and arrogance are palpable dangers, so are sloth and lethargy. Of these two pairs, pride and arrogance are the pair that is generally highlighted; sloth and lethargy are all too often ignored. Both pairs are manifestations of human sinfulness.

The couple coping with cystic fibrosis do not have to go in a technological direction. They do not have to choose against any embryos or future individuals with cystic fibrosis. The availability of the technology does not make any particular way forward inevitable (unless society foists one or other direction on them). But they do have to choose, and they do have to live with the repercussions and consequences of their choices. These could include children with cystic fibrosis, children without cystic fibrosis, and embryos and fetuses that will develop no further and so will never live as children suffering from cystic fibrosis. The couple having to make these invidious choices can never escape from one or other of these consequences, because they (and we) are creatures who live in community.

As with so many similar areas, the dimensions of the situation are constantly changing. Advances in medical treatment have meant that those with cystic fibrosis can now live longer lives and ones of higher quality than would have been the case just a few years ago. This, of course, is true only if the resources and facilities are both available and affordable. But this gives hope where there may have been despair, and it may influence the choices that are made before birth. This is encouraging, but it has to be remembered that it is only made possible by advances in medical technology and by increases in human abilities to control disease processes.

Searching for motifs

But wait, you may say. Don't put couples like this into this predicament. Wouldn't it be far better if we left well alone and refused to go in these technological directions? Concerns about humans playing God stem from a fear that humans are acquiring too many powers, powers they might seriously misuse. The underlying assumption is that they need not enter into these realms. Why not accept what nature brings, or what God brings, depending on one's perspective? No matter how the question is phrased, the basic assumption is that the only truly responsible route to take is to leave well enough alone. There is virtue in ignorance; there is something good about a lack of control; there is something of merit in mystery and in the unknown.

If we wind back the clock of this scenario far enough, we will come to a time when there was no amniocentesis and no gene probes for cystic fibrosis, no PGD and no means of fertilising embryos in the laboratory. Surely these were halcyon days, with little decision-making, no destruction of embryos, and no abortions for therapeutic reasons.

Any serious arguments along these lines are doing little more than seeking refuge from decision-making in an enclave of ignorance and disease. The couple in question would be left having to cope with one or more children dying from cystic fibrosis in childhood. The so-called "ideal" means young lives blighted by tragically foreshortened existences. While this might not be the ultimate of tragedies, and while children like this can bring profound blessings and joy to some families, is there any virtue in suffering from cystic fibrosis if there are ways in which this situation can be ameliorated? As we have just seen, advances in its treatment have made huge differences to the lives of those with cystic fibrosis (and for their families), and yet this has been brought about by medical advance – not by sitting back and letting nature takes its course.

These are quite fundamental issues because they force us to come to terms with our picture of God and God's domain. How much do we leave to God, and how much is it legitimate for us to do? Do we simply sit back and let God sort everything out, or has he given us the responsibility, authority and power to sort out much for ourselves, and even in his name? Indeed, what does it mean to say that we are leaving everything to God? Is this anything more than taking a fatalistic stance, but packaging it in apparently pious language?

The foundation for my thinking is that humans are to exercise dominion over nature, and that we are to free ourselves from its constraints. In carrying out these mandates we are to act as good stewards of God's creation, realising that there is much in his creation that is not as it should be. Andrew Dutney (2001) has expressed it forcefully like this:

> Nature disappoints. It lets us down. Nature sometimes fails to serve the good. Indeed it sometimes generates evil. And it is a

horrible irony that sometimes even human conception amounts to the generation of evil. In such circumstances of brokenness, it is not the human vocation to acquiesce but, by grace and in the strength of the Holy Spirit, to give expression to such freedom as is available by exercising dominion over nature.

It is interesting that Dutney here uses the word "nature", and not the word "God". Replace nature with God, and it is obvious why he does this. Does God disappoint? Does he let us down? Does he sometimes fail to serve the good? Does he generate evil? Christians will answer "no" to each of these questions, and quite rightly so. In other words, the problems lie in the natural world, and in those aspects of it that tear us apart, the diseases that detract from the wholeness of our lives, whether genetic or viral in origin, the natural catastrophes that destroy and maim, and the ugliness of deformity and dashed expectations. An investigation into the causes of so much disharmony and strife lies beyond the scope of this book. My concern is with the reality that confronts all of us in every community, and the question from which we cannot escape: what are we to do?

There are no easy answers, since we frequently have to live with ambiguity and uncertainty. We are torn in different directions, often not knowing which is the best course of action. We may well not know which way is pleasing to God, or which way will best serve other human beings. No wonder many long for a world in which such choices don't have to be made.

Let me return to the couple with cystic fibrosis in the family to see where further reflection on their situation may lead us. If the couple consent to any of their embryos being destroyed, it is because these particular embryos carry a gene that will result in children with cystic fibrosis. Either way, they are confronted by an agonising moral choice – whether to dispose of the embryos, or to have them implanted in the wife's uterus knowing that a resulting child will suffer from a debilitating disease. The easy, and possibly morally preferable, way out of this dilemma is via ignorance; they are unaware of the options and can do nothing about them. They are shielded from making a difficult, and possibly invidious, decision; they will have to take what comes. This is precisely the position in which we repeatedly find ourselves, and yet we usually regard this as a position of weakness rather than of strength. Ignorance is not a virtue when confronted by malaria, tuber-culosis or dysentery, or by measles or smallpox – all of which are diseases that we can do something about. In these instances, knowledge is preferable to ignorance, although in the earlier part of the 20th century ignorance reigned supreme.

If we opt for knowledge over ignorance, a choice between human embryos and the health status of future children has to be made in cases such as this. At a more general level, research on human embryos raises similar issues, where the anticipated outcome of the research, albeit some distance into the future, is the improvement of human health. The general thrust of acting as God's stewards comes into play here as well. There are two possible courses of action, both of which have problematic elements. This is where Christians (as well as others within the community) reach different conclusions, since specific biblical teaching and precise theological guid-ance are unavailable. A common approach is to seek a defini-tive answer to the question of when human life (personhood) begins. However, as the case of cystic fibrosis illustrates, the ethical dilemma emerges out of the choice that has to be made – between the interests of early embryos and those of children and subsequently adults who will have a potentially serious medical condition. To greater or lesser degrees this will always be the choice.

Simple solutions will probably bypass this choice, since they will concentrate on one party or one interest, to the exclusion of all others directly or indirectly affected. In order to do justice to a range of theological motifs, a number of guiding principles will have to be consulted and balanced. These will not provide definitive answers, but hopefully they will enable us to construct a helpful forum within which to debate the respective merits of contending forces.

The *first motif* is provided by the urge to restore the material world: to improve it, care for it, and cure those with distressing conditions. Inevitably, our attention is on human beings in need of medical help and assistance. If there are current or imminent scientific measures that might realistically be able to alleviate serious illnesses, under normal circumstances they should be pursued. This should be within the bounds of a balanced lifestyle and broad overall interests, and also the character of all those involved in decision-making. How do they live, and how will the decisions that have to be made enrich and extend their lives as human beings?

A *second motif* is that we are to be guided by the relationships that make up the human community. Decisions made in any one area may influence human relationships in other areas, and also our attitudes towards human life in general. Will they enhance or detract from the value bestowed on prenatal or post-natal human life, the disabled, the marginalised, and the chronically ill? There are no clear-cut answers to these queries, and answers may vary in different situations. Once again, delicate decision-making is imperative.

A *third motif* revolves around the context of the embryos implicated in decision-making. So much of the debate about the moral status of human embryos assumes that embryos can be viewed as isolated entities. This is deeply misleading, since their status is intimately dependent upon the environment in which they exist, and the communities of which they are a part (see Chapter 3). And so, when a disease like cystic fibrosis is present, it has to be asked whether this can best be tackled at the embryonic stage, or later on in fetal or more likely post-natal life. Each of these stages may be relevant, but is one preferable to another on ethical and/or clinical grounds? What is preferable for one couple may not be for another couple, and even the answer one couple give at one time may not be the answer they would give at another time.

The frequently expressed concern is that the destruction of human life, even at its very earliest stages, will lead to an objectification of human life. While there is nothing inevitable about this, the mere possibility reminds us that any destruction of human life, or even any use of human tissue following a tragedy, has to be undertaken with extreme care. Awareness that human powers can be used in manipulatory ways should instil caution into our grand ventures. Human dignity can be readily sacrificed in the pursuit of meagre ends. What is needed is a balancing perspective. All those participating in, and affected by, therapeutic decision-making are human beings; hence, our horizon has to extend beyond embryos alone. Acknowledging this is not meant to lead to a downgrading of embryonic status, but is simply a reminder that post-natal human beings can be held hostage by unduly elevating rudimentary human life. No one direction is self-evidently more appropriate either theologically or ethically. It is imperative that we work through the issues in each individual situation. Judgement and discernment are mandatory.

A *fourth motif* is that human life is not an absolute, in that it can be taken or sacrificed for what is considered to be a higher good (as in war or martyrdom). In the same way, some early embryonic life could possibly be sacrificed to make possible therapeutic developments with vast potential benefits for many sections of humanity. Any justification for sacrificing embryos in this way stems from the good that is thought to emerge from research on certain embryos, or replacing only "healthy" embryos in the case of serious genetic diseases. Any argument along these lines need not presuppose that early human embryos have an inferior status to that of postnatal humans; it lies in the balancing of goods, as is done most clearly in war (where those killed are definitely human and yet their deaths are considered justifiable in terms of the overall objectives of the conflicts). The dominant consideration is to determine what will best serve the interests of children and adults, and whether this can be justified alongside the sacrifice of embryos (see Chapter 3).

For Christians there is also a *fifth motif*, namely, one's dependence upon God. While a global principle like this will not immediately answer the sort of very specific questions with which I am concerned, it is the fundamental relationship that is the bedrock for all these considerations. The couple with cystic fibrosis in their family should be guided in all their decisions by their dependence on God. This will help them come to terms with the agonies and trauma of the ambivalence implicit within their moral decision-making. Where there are no "correct" answers, there are answers that demonstrate faithfulness to one's relationship to God and one's position within a community of the Lord's people. While different individuals, couples and groups will reach different conclusions, the questions that need to be asked are whether these conclusions have been arrived at "before God" and whether their actions are as "unto the Lord".

We must play God

In view of this discussion, what are we to make of the decisions reached by the couples in the six illustrations with which I commenced this chapter?

Illustration 1: Geoff and Cindy were indeed playing God, even though they had a baby by perfectly natural means. In the eyes of most people, they were playing God in the best way possible. Most would not even use the term "playing God" in this instance. Geoff and Cindy were acting naturally, although this is not strictly accurate since they were using contraceptives, which would be regarded by some as introducing an artificial element into their sexual relationship. However, apart from this, even this example of playing God can go abysmally wrong and can be carried out with foul intentions and in an immoral and unspiritual context. There is nothing assured even about having a baby by what most would regard as perfectly natural means.

Illustration 2: Does the artificial element of IVF convert childbirth into an unworthy endeavour? The motives of Luke and Carrie were exemplary. I would argue they were not overstepping the bounds of this dominion, even though they were extending the boundaries of the natural process. Opinions differ even here, though, and not all will accept this procedure as readily as I do. Objections to this process tend to centre on the legitimacy or otherwise of separating the sexual and procreative aspects of reproduction. This takes us into different territory, and if it is regarded as a legitimate objection, there is no room for any artificial intervention in the reproductive process. However, this objection does not usually have anything to do with playing God, since it is far more specifically focused on reproduction. There are other objections to IVF that see it as the thin end of the wedge; once interference is allowed here for apparently good reasons, there is no stopping what can be done to embryos in the laboratory. My response is that we have to use moral discernment to make judgments of this nature, and that this is not a convincing argument against employing IVF for a couple such as the one envisaged in this illustration.

Illustration 3: The social element in the use of IVF takes the situation of Graeme and his ballerina partner, Amanda, a step further. What has to be taken into account here is the whole context of their lives as human beings, and the place and timing of childbirth within this context. Different couples would make quite different decisions if confronted by this choice, although the whole process still fits within normal bio-logical parameters. The challenge of this illustration is to take account of the place of wider relationships that impact upon the reproductive sphere. There is no doubt that this couple are using an artificial process to meet social and family needs in the absence of any therapeutic imperative. As such, the action in this case falls outside the stress that I normally lay upon the importance of a therapeutic context. But consider this: if they acted in this manner without resorting to IVF it would arouse little comment on the part of most people. If child-bearing can be put off for two or five years, why not for ten or fifteen years? This is generally considered acceptable, any issues that do arise being biological ones. Is there then any significant difference between this semi-natural situation and the far less natural one of the couple in this illustration? It is a matter of degree. Personally, I would urge couples to think very seriously before acting like Graeme and Amanda, simply because they are pushing the limits of the biological for social reasons. Nevertheless, I would not wish to condemn their actions.

Illustration 4: Sex selection has daunting overtones of

social control, and one would need to know why Greg and Bronwyn wanted to move in this direction. There are some sex-linked genetic conditions for which a strong case can be made for implanting embryos of a particular sex. Other reasons tend to be far less substantial, and serious problems are beginning to emerge here. However, talk of "designer babies" doesn't promote valuable discussion. This couple are taking a socially-driven artificial approach much further than in the previous illustration. The costs, both financial and technological, are high, making this a deeply troubling venture. Any reasons brought forward to justify it would have to be compelling; far more compelling than the one set forth in the illustration. People have always wanted a child of one sex rather than another, but the simple longing for a boy or girl is generally regarded as ephemeral. Any longing of this nature does not justify going to unusual lengths to satisfy it. The financial cost cannot be justified; surely the money could be put to better use. The same applies for the technology; why waste technological resources in this way? This couple appear to be giving no thought to broader communal interests.

Illustration 5: A host of social and biological controls predominate in the case of Mike and 60-year-old Sally, and doubts arise over the welfare of the resulting child. Even here there are no hard and fast rules, and simply labelling this "playing God" doesn't help. However, any move in this direction is injudicious and probably unwarranted. This illustration has similar connotations to those of the previous two. What we encounter in these three cases is a spectrum of social interference in natural reproduction, from the least invasive (illustration 3) to the most invasive (illustrations 4 and 5). Similar considerations apply to those in illustration 4, making this a highly dubious venture. While I am not prepared to state that Mike and Sally are wrong in acting like this, I would recommend against it, on the ground that it is pushing biological parameters to the limits, and because it appears to be giving little thought to the offspring and therefore to family interests.

Illustration 6: The situation presented by Paul and Simone, with its altruistic surrogacy, raises fewer difficulties than do the previous illustrations. Biologically few boundaries are being crossed, and if all parties accept what is being done, and if the resulting child will be cared for and loved, and will be informed later of its origins, the problems are probably less severe than often imagined. What is crucial here is the depth and integrity of the relationships of all involved. It is unfortunate that surrogacy is usually seen in commercial terms, with all the potential pitfalls of any financial transaction. What the altruistic version brings to the fore is the importance of family relationships and the community within which the family is located. This is why instances of altruistic surrogacy stand or fall on the strength of these relationships. While enormous care, together with focused counselling and legal direction, is essential, this may be a way forward in some instances. Whether or not it involves IVF, it can be an example of altruism at its best.

In all these illustrations, the people concerned are meddling in and with God's world. Whether or not their actions are justified depends on a host of other factors. There is a continuum from natural childbirth at one end through to surrogacy or post-menopausal childbirth at the other. Numerous ethical and theological issues arise in some of these cases, all of which have to be assessed on their own terms. What shines through is an intimate intertwining of ethical, social and theological threads, and it is the untangling of these that is the spiritual task of human beings who are made in the image of God.

Should we be meddling in God's world? While the word

"meddling" is loaded with negative overtones, denoting as it does interference in something, we should be actively promoting and contributing to God's world. This is involvement, rather than interference, in the world he has brought into existence. As creatures brought into this world by God, our task is to enhance the world of which we are a part, and the well-being of those among whom we live. I am arguing that this is a Christian duty. The challenge is to determine how to implement this duty.

Chapter 2

Designer Babies: Who is the Designer?

The term "designer babies" is one of those terms beloved by sections of the media and the popular press, and it is generally used negatively. Designing babies is one of the things we should not do, because it is going too far. For Christians this means doing something that should be left in the hands of God, where it rightfully belongs. No one with even a modicum of common sense, let alone spiritual discernment, would countenance the idea. It is playing God in the negative sense outlined in the last chapter, because the design of babies is a clear manifestation of playing God in a foolhardy manner.

In my view, dismissing bioethical issues in this way helps no one, and it certainly fails to answer any of the major ethical and theological questions that confront us with increasing vigour and complexity each week. We have to dig much deeper. Christians, in particular, should be searching for good reasons for why we approve of some projects and disapprove of others. The last things we should be content with are slogans.

What do we mean when we talk about designing babies?

The central problem with this debate is its unrealistic nature, based as it is on a set of *misleading images* of the notion of what designing a human being might entail, and on a serious lack of appreciation of the state of genetic science. The ease with which the term "designer baby" is employed is matched only by a fear of the ever-increasing scientific control of some humans over the nascent lives of other humans. Are human beings becoming far too efficient in their manipulatory abilities, and are they leaving far too little to chance or to divine control?

Those who readily refer to designing babies are equally free in their references to *making babies to order*. And the implication is that if babies are made to order they will subsequently be treated as little more than *impersonal products*. After all, this is what design is all about: the more precise and sophisticated the design, the more effective and acceptable the product will be. Provide the specifications of what you want, and that is what you will be provided with. Add a few ingredients and omit a few others, and the resulting product will have been designed to suit your likes and dislikes, your whims, your lifestyle, and your aspirations.

It is but a short step from here to the dubiously fascinating and repulsive picture of the factory production of babies. This comes to the fore in connection with human reproductive cloning, with its routinely presented pictures of babies being spewed out of machines in endless identical lines, as though they were newspapers, pills or soft-drink bottles. Such pictures are, of course, deeply disconcerting and we quite naturally recoil from them (Jones, 2001). The trouble is that these provocative and grossly misleading images, with their oppressive overtones of a manufacturing process, are all too readily applied to any genetic intervention in embryos – change one gene, or discard one embryo in favour of another, and the result is a designer baby. The intended message is that all such babies are no more than factory-produced, impersonal products. But is this true? Whether or not it is the case, simplistic general statements like this do nothing to advance serious debate.

The production of a particular model of automobile is characterised by precision, equivalence and uniformity. There is no room for individuality on the production line, since each car has to conform to the specifications of that model. When I buy a car I expect it to perform exactly like all other examples of that particular model; the last thing I expect or want is for it to have interesting quirks of its own that no one had ever predicted and no one is capable of rectifying. Neither do I expect it to change its character as each year passes. To use a biological analogy, its manufacture is entirely genetic in character; there is no environmental component, since no further development can take place once it has come off the production line. If the cloning of human beings or any genetic intervention were to result in such reproducibility, we would be rightly alarmed. But there is a problem with this analogy. It overlooks something important, and this is the environmental component that is always present in the production and subsequent development of human beings – whether cloned or naturally fertilised, and it is this that separates human reproduction (even with impersonal elements) from factory manufacturing processes.

The environment is implicit in all biological development, but it plays no part in physical manufacturing processes. In this sense, biological manufacture is a misnomer. We will never produce babies in the same way as we produce cars, washing machines or computers, even if we set out to do so. These analogies are, therefore, seriously misleading. If the notion of design involves precision and predictability, there is no way in which babies and future human individuals will ever be designed by people like us. This in no way justifies all the procedures in the artificial reproductive technologies, but it should make us careful that we are not misled by the terminology we use.

What then about the *science*? Once again, there are problems. So often the focus appears to be on choosing genes for fair hair, blue eyes, intelligence, physique and good looks, or avoiding baldness, or whatever. The ephemeral nature of these longings serves only to demonstrate their superficiality, not to mention an ignorance of the scientific precision, clinical complexities and expensive resources that would be required to achieve them. Unfortunately, instead of demythologising such fantasies as empty claims, they are taken seriously and are used to construct tirades against realistic and therapeutically based genetic choice. The latter can then be dismissed on the ground that its goal is that of producing perfect babies, designed to order.

You will notice that yet another theme has crept in here, and this is *perfectibility*. Once more, this conveys powerful negative overtones. It is, of course, a theological theme, not a scientific one. There is no way in which science can bring about perfection at any level, even in basic biological functioning. Certainly it may be able to help restore reasonably normal functioning, and this is what we normally look for. But what is perfection in scientific terms? Generally, that is seen as a meaningless question. Perfection is not an objective or a neutral concept, since it reflects our ideals, our goals and our longings. It is what we would like to see. And so as far as babies are concerned, it is the sort of babies (and one hopes future individuals) we want: healthy, intelligent, deaf (in some deaf communities), or athletic. There is no one version of perfection, since each version reflects our own predilections.

Unfortunately, once these obvious points are overlooked and perfection is a mantle foisted onto science, one ends up with a most unfortunate message, that science has almost redemptive powers. Once this is even hinted at, people begin to think that salvation can be found in biological manipulation, and that the hope of a better life can emanate from genetic intervention. This is a grotesque mixing up of science and theology, taking us well beyond the powers of science (either now or in the future). It is a distortion of the character of science, and in turn it casts a shadow over the legitimate contributions of genetic science. Too often the baby of legitimate science is thrown out with the bathwater of contorted images of science as saviour and bringer of all good things.

What is required is a rigorous assessment of the merits of what can and cannot be accomplished by genetic science. We need to ask what can be realistically accomplished to benefit ordinary people. This should be our starting point, with its focus on the good of the person, with a commitment to improve the quality of the person's life and, if feasible, to replace illness by health. This is a positive hope, but it is also a realistic one. The genetic intervention may not work; hopes may be dashed. But the attempt is to be encouraged as long as our expectations are guided by realistic clinical and scientific goals. There is no hint here of perfection or of ageless existence in a disease-free body. The dominant virtues are those of humility (Philippians 2:5–8), demonstrated by caring for those in need, and of utilising powerful technologies in the service of those potentially capable of benefiting from them.

Genetic manipulation of embryos

If design in a purely factory-production sense is not to be contemplated, where does this leave us when it comes to the genetic manipulation of embryos? This is much closer to a realistic view of the current status of biomedical science, and also of how it might develop in the foreseeable future.

Starting in the present day, let's consider pre-implantation genetic diagnosis (PGD), as currently practised. As outlined in the last chapter, this is a procedure devised to test early human embryos for serious inherited genetic conditions. Only embryos that are free from the condition are transferred to a woman, in the expectation that a normal pregnancy will develop. Inevitably, this involves selecting embryos: selecting those that are not genetic carriers of the disease trait, and discarding those that have the gene responsible for the disease.

I am aware that the selection of embryos like this is anathema to some people, since some embryos are being accepted and others rejected. Regarding the individual embryos involved, some are being selected for life and others are being selected for destruction. For those to whom all embryos are human persons (in the sense in which those of us reading these words are human persons, and all embryos are to be treated as having equal value), no embryos should ever be selected against. While I take up this point in Chapter 4, it is worth thinking of the place of selection in other areas of our lives. Selection takes place when we select one school over another for our children; selection occurs in adoption when a child with one set of characteristics is selected over one with another set; selection is evident when we select one person to be our partner rather than another. These and many other instances of selection affect the lives of other human beings (sometimes detrimentally), and yet we regard them as ethically and theologically valid. Selecting student A over student B for a highly sought-after university course will have implications for both students, and perhaps negative ones for student B. Similarly, selecting patient C over patient D to have an expensive and much needed operation may result in extending the life (or quality of life) of C but not that of D.

Nevertheless, we consider this acceptable as long as the criteria underlying the selection are valid and equitable. Hence, selection per se should not be used as a weapon against the selection of one embryo over another.

PGD, which was first developed in 1990, is used for three different types of abnormality. First, single-gene disorders that cause conditions like cystic fibrosis and Huntington's disease; second, familial sex-linked disorders, such as hemophilia and Duchenne's muscular dystrophy; and third, familial chromosomal disorders, such as various forms of translocation. In addition, there is aneuploidy screening for specific numerical chromosomal disorders, including Down's syndrome and Turner's syndrome (ESHRE, 2002; Cochrane Menstrual Disorders and Subfertility Group, 2004). A drawback of PGD is that it can be used only in conjunction with IVF. In other words, fertilisation has to take place in the laboratory using IVF, even when IVF is not required on the grounds of infertility.

One of the features of PGD is that it enables the sex of embryos to be readily determined. This is both an advantage and a disadvantage. The advantage is that, when dealing with sex-linked genetic conditions such as hemophilia and Duchenne's muscular dystrophy, it enables embryos of the appropriate sex to be selected so that the resulting child will not suffer from the condition in question. This is exactly what is required. The disadvantage is that sex selection can be used for spurious social control of the next generation, by providing parents with a child of the preferred sex. This form of sex selection has nothing to do with anything medical or therapeutic.

Some people refer to babies born after PGD as designer babies, since there is interference at a very early stage of their development. As should have become clear from the preceding section, this is not design in any meaningful sense, even though choices are being made between embryos. But, in terms of design, the choice is a crude one. Whenever I buy a jacket and decide that *this* jacket is preferable to *that* jacket, I have not suddenly become a fashion designer. All I have done is make a selection from the two that are available. PGD is similar, even if somewhat more sophisticated. The design component is negligible. Of course, we do not have to travel in this direction, and PGD does not have to be undertaken. However, once an appropriate procedure is available, choices are inevitably being made, even if the decision is to refrain from using the procedure. The nature of these choices emerged in the last chapter.

This is fine, but there are already indications that PGD can be used in a far more radical fashion than anything I have just mentioned. After all, we now hear about "saviour siblings", where one baby is brought into the world in an attempt to save the life of an already existing sibling. Surely this is doing nothing more than using the one child for the benefit of the other child, and this is exploitation of the worst kind. On the surface that sounds like an eminently sensible response, and it is definitely one we should not dismiss without giving it serious attention. Technically, this is human leukocyte antigen (HLA) tissue-typing, which is an additional step to PGD to determine if an embryo could lead to the birth of a child who is a tissue match for an ill sibling. PGD is used to select embryos free of the familial disorder in question, and the only embryos implanted are those that are a tissue match to the older sibling and are free of this disorder. At birth, the umbilical cord blood of this child is used to treat the older sibling.

If there were any hint that the saviour sibling was not going to be valued as a unique and valuable individual in his or her own right, then concerns about this form of tissue typing would undoubtedly be justified. Hence, any thoughts about "using" this child as the source of bone marrow, or even of a kidney or other organ, raise deep concerns. On the other hand, if this child is loved and treated as a person to be respected and valued just as much as any other member of the family, then there may be a place for HLA tissue-typing in some instances. However, once a child is valued in this way, the ways in which he or she will be used in the interests of others will be circumscribed. In Christian terms, both the original child and the saviour sibling are made in the image of God and are of equal worth in his sight; as such, we too should value them equally.

A further use to which PGD may be put is to avoid the implantation of an embryo with a late-onset genetic disorder such as Huntington's disease or an embryo with a predisposition to develop conditions like diabetes, high blood pressure or breast cancer (Human Genetics Commission, 2004). These are the sorts of issues that I touch on in the next section.

More generally, PGD also raises issues about our attitudes towards those who have disabilities. Some argue that it discriminates against people with disabilities and promotes the view that the birth of people with disabilities should be prevented (Parker *et al.*, 2002; Nelson, 2003). The concern here is that if embryos with genetic disorders are screened out, society in general will become more prejudiced against disabled people. While these concerns cannot be ignored, because public attitudes can be swayed to put pressure on couples to use PGD or have abortions to avoid the birth of children with minor abnormalities, an important distinction has to be made. This is between "disability" and "people with disabilities". Selecting against embryos with severe genetic disorders does not necessarily imply that the lives of people with disabilities (genetic or as a result of injury) are any less valuable or meaningful than the lives of those without such disabilities. From a Christian perspective this distinction is of immense significance, since our dealings are mainly with people, and it is people who bear God's image and are to be related to as one with us in the human community. Whether embryos are equally part of this community is a contentious issue that is taken up in Chapter 3.

Genetic manipulation in the future: Therapy or enhancement?

Against this background, let us move into the future and into the realm of the hypothetical and the speculative. Here I envisage what uses might one day be made of PGD. Consider this: an embryo can be tested for the presence of a gene responsible for some forms of Alzheimer's disease (AD); in practice, this may be a set of interacting genes. This makes it possible to predict that some embryos have a vastly increased chance of developing AD by the age of 60 years. Let's also imagine that gene therapy has now reached a stage where this AD-causing gene can be replaced by a normal gene, without giving rise to deleterious side-effects. The end result of these actions is to decrease very considerably the likelihood that this future individual will suffer from AD. Another very similar scenario is provided by genetic manipulation of embryos as a means of decreasing the chance of these individuals developing heart disease at 50 years of age.

In these cases, no embryos have been discarded, and so there has been no choice between embryos. However, the embryos have been modified, and so in this sense have been designed. Actually, they have been designed to a far greater extent than anything contemplated using current procedures. The babies who result will, in a real sense, be designer babies, in that the individuals later in life will be considerably different from what they would have been like in the absence of the modification. Even this, of course, is nothing like true factory design, since only one facet of the embryo, and hence individual, has been modified.

Consider another futuristic example. In this instance, it is known that, unless something is done to the embryo, the future individual will suffer from mental retardation. Suppose that it is possible to make use of gene therapy in the embryo to produce an individual without mental retardation. This takes gene therapy much further, since the manipulated individual will be radically different from early infancy onwards. This is truly "improving" the life of an individual, since what it amounts to is a dramatic transformation of this person's life. And this, again, would be a designer baby.

The principle here is the same as in the AD and heart disease examples, but the repercussions for the future individual are far greater. The design element here is far more powerful and the repercussions are far more dramatic. But the treatment is aimed at improving the life of the individual. Should design of this type be condemned, if it ever proves possible to achieve something as far-reaching as what I have hypothesised? This would take us into the realm of gene therapy.

I am not advocating that we even contemplate moving in any of these directions, but I believe there is merit in at least beginning to think seriously about thought experiments of this type. What we have in them is genetic manipulation of a high order, but it is manipulation that would (if everything worked out as hoped) improve the life of the individuals into which these embryos would develop. Of course, one can debate whether it would be improvement, and the scientific aspects would be anything but simple. Indeed, they would probably prove to be very complex and very expensive, and would pose innumerable challenges. They might also cause as many problems as they solve. And they would not rid the world of AD, heart problems and mental retardation.

All I am saying is that, in the same way as normal brain function is preferable to epileptic fits, or normal kidney function is preferable to kidney failure or nephritis, perhaps we should not dismiss out of hand means (including genetic means) of remedying major defects. Remember, though, if we agree with this possibility we are agreeing to the partial design, or at least modification, of embryos. On the other hand, if we reject these ventures out of hand, we are also rejecting in principle what could amount to radical forms of therapy. Neither course of action is self-evidently correct, and both merit very serious thought. Arguments need to be marshalled for and against each possibility, so that the inevitable losses and gains on both sides can be balanced against one another.

Striving for balance in this manner is a reminder that a choice is being made. This is between "design plus therapy" and "no design and no therapy". The therapeutic possibilities are linked closely to the ability to impose some design on nascent human beings. As we have already seen, the design element is rudimentary, but its complete absence holds out little or no hope of therapeutic developments based on genetic manipulation. This contrast does not predicate going in any particular direction, but it does highlight the consequences of the choices being made.

A notable feature of these futuristic illustrations is that they incorporate an *enhancement* element, and enhancement is one of those phenomena that send shivers down the spines of many people. But what is enhancement? So often it is the idea that a healthy person, whom I shall call H, will be enhanced so that they become super-healthy (SH). They will be more intelligent than they would have been; they will be able to argue more convincingly, or think more quickly; or they may be able to run much faster and hear wavelengths previously beyond their capabilities. In other words, instead of correcting defects, which is the realm of therapy, normal functions will be extended, taking us into the realm of enhancement. Against this background, we have to ask whether the individuals in my examples are H or SH. They are not SH in that they are vulnerable to almost the whole range of usual diseases; their only protection is against early onset AD, heart disease or mental retardation respectively. In no sense do they represent some new form of human being. They may be healthier than they would have been in the absence of the gene therapy (we may call them H+ individuals), but even here the various forms of therapy may have side effects that detract from their postulated advantages. In other words, enhancement is not as different from therapy as it is so often depicted.

While it would be unwise to get too carried away with far-reaching hypothetical possibilities like these, by the same token we need a framework that can take account of dramatic new directions that medical therapy might take. If we lack such a framework, we will simply reject the possibility of any new directions, or accept everything that comes along. Let us consider what such a framework might look like.

Constructing a framework for genetic intervention

It might be helpful to sketch the rough parameters of a framework as a basis for further thinking in this area. These might include the following:

- An *openness to genetic ventures* incorporating embryonic manipulation as acceptable, on the condition that the means employed have the potential to enhance the dignity or personal status of the individuals concerned. Such a therapeutic context is *person-centred*, and stresses that the welfare of individuals is paramount. Genetic therapy and genetic modification are to be used to assist people in need, and not to satisfy ventures of hyperbole.

- A *therapeutic context* serves to control and limit scientific bravado. While it does not provide an infallible framework, it sets itself against one in which the ultimate goal is the creation of a race of supermen and superwomen. This is the contrast between therapy and hubris. To use genetic interventions to serve the aspirations of those wanting perfect children or idealised offspring is to misconstrue the science and misappropriate a therapeutic context. No matter what the technological ventures, the focus should always be on the welfare of people.

- There is always a *continuum* from unremarkable therapy at one end through to startling new therapeutic possibilities at the other. Failure to acknowledge this continuum has two possible repercussions. Those who are fearful will oppose all forms of genetic science; those who are filled with bravado will seek to use the power of genetic science for self-aggrandisement. Both responses are problematic, in that both overlook what might be available to assist those in need. Recognition of the continuum offers a productive middle way that provides a constructive base for Christian responses.

- Science is *not omnipotent*, and even the degree of understanding and control I have hypothesised is unrealistic. All human control and all human expertise are severely limited, these limitations stemming from a mixture of finiteness and evil intentions. It would be a tragedy if our assessment of genetic science became warped by false illusions of scientific power. A backlash against such arrogance leads to rejection of any use of genetics therapeutically. This, in turn, may cause us to turn our backs on abilities made available to us by God.

- Genetics in *isolation* provides a limited understanding of what constitutes the human person. It has to be seen alongside the environment within which individuals develop and function. It is this interaction between genetic and environmental factors that is basic to everything we are as people. This in no way invalidates the significance of genetics, but it does serve to place it within a broader biological context.

- Genetics raises issues for the *community*, and society at large, as well as for individuals. While my emphasis has been on individuals and therapy, broader issues are also relevant, including the availability of resources to benefit the wider community, and the role of justice and equity in ensuring that genetic advances are used across relevant sections of the community. It is also important to stipulate that the availability of genetic knowledge does not jeopardise the personal integrity of groups within the community.

- The human person is always susceptible to *manipulation* – behaviourally, politically, pharmacologically and, in rare instances, genetically. There is no escape from this, since relationships with others are central to human existence, and these demonstrate the ease with which we abuse and exploit others for base ends. This emphasis on relationships stems from what we are as persons made in the image of a triune God. Relationships are central to the functioning of the Godhead, and to every facet of human existence – biologically as well as spiritually. Issues raised by genetic advance are far from new ones, reiterating as they do issues and problems with a long history.

Cloning – the epitome of design?

One of the prevailing fears for many is that the cloning of individuals, or reproductive cloning, will lead to offspring who have been designed by their progenitors. They will not be allowed to be themselves because they will have been brought into the world to be like someone else, to walk in the footsteps of someone who has already existed. Human clones will have been deliberately designed to suit the purposes of someone else. Consequently, reproductive cloning is frequently viewed as the epitome of all that is wrong with designing people. Almost by definition it imperils human dignity and so is inherently tainted (examples are provided by Kass, 1998).

From what I have already said, this viewpoint should strike us as dubious. It is difficult to understand how producing someone like me can be described as designing someone. It is attempting to replicate me in certain important ways, but it is replicating my weaknesses as well as my strengths, and my ill health as well as my good health (inasmuch as these are genetically based). There is no attempt to improve upon what I have been; it is simply attempting to repeat me in another generation. Even this replication will prove inadequate, because cloning takes no account of environmental influences. For instance, cloning JOHN DOBBS will result in the production of his clone, john dobbs. However, what will result will not be john dobbs, but john dobbs (M), a modified version of john dobbs. Hence, even if the intention of cloning JOHN DOBBS was to produce his exact replica (albeit in another generation), the resulting john dobbs (M) would be quite unlike the original in many significant ways. The similarities would be greater than found in mark dobbs, the natural son of JOHN DOBBS, but they would sorely disappoint anyone who expected to be confronted by a second version of the original JOHN DOBBS.

Nevertheless, one of the major arguments against the cloning of human individuals emanates from the design motif. With this in mind, let us look briefly at the design-related concerns (more general concerns are dealt with in Chapter 6).

The first is the concern that cloned individuals will be *instrumentalised*, since they will be treated as objects and not as people; things to be exchanged, bought and sold in the market place. This is the way in which we treat inanimate objects that have been designed, and yet we do not have to design objects or people to treat them like this. In ordinary life parents sometimes make children instruments of their own ambitions. This is instrumentalisation, but there is no hint here of design in a biological sense.

Regardless of whether children are conceived naturally or artificially, they should be accepted for who they are and loved for who they are (Jones, 2001). Existence must be in the best interests of the child, who must then be given the freedom to develop as a unique individual. Unfortunately, some clones would probably be treated in an instrumental fashion, but by the same token others probably would not. In other words, the way in which people are treated depends on a host of factors, only one of which may be the manner in which they were brought into existence.

A second concern, which may be more directly applicable

to the possibility of design, is the possibility, or even inevitability, that a clone would be forced to *walk in the footsteps of another* (Jonas, 1978). It is argued that excessive demands would be placed on clones by parents or genotype donors to ensure that they lived up to a set of preconceived expectations – to be exactly like "daddy" or "mummy" (or a famous individual?). These are legitimate concerns, and yet they rely largely on carrying out the cloning for egotistical reasons. To force a clone to walk in another's footsteps would primarily be accomplished behaviourally rather than biologically. Behavioural cloning, where excessive demands are placed on individuals or groups to perform to certain expectations in, say, sporting, artistic or church circles, is no more justifiable in these circles than it would be in cloning. It would be tyrannical of a progenitor to try and determine another's fate in this way. However, in a healthy family and social environment, this would be unlikely; one might actually learn from the progenitor's life.

A third concern is that clones' *lack of genetic uniqueness* would deprive them of their uniqueness as individuals (Kahn, 1997). The assumption underlying this is that our freedom resides in the genetic lottery and in genetic uncertainty, and in the unpredictability of our genetic combinations (Meilaender, 1998). To do away with such unpredictability is, it is claimed, akin to imposing on clones the predictability of a designed unit (see Chapter 1).

Implicit within this concern is the fundamental assumption that our uniqueness as individuals stems entirely from our genetic uniqueness. However, identical twins demonstrate unequivocally that whatever the relationship is between human and genetic uniqueness, it is not a direct one. Similarly, clones with (almost) identical genetic make-up would have different brains. This is because the organisation of the brain is as much dependent on soft wiring (influenced by the environment) as on hard wiring (built-in genetically). Environmental influences are not mere afterthoughts or unimportant peripheral add-ons, but are essential for the final form of any brain. Our identity is shaped by the history of our relations with others, and by our biographies.

By itself, a lack of genetic uniqueness cannot be a threat to our freedom (Jones, 2001). Additional factors forcing us to conform to the whims of other people are required. These would involve forcing us to see what they want us to see, reading what they want us to read, viewing the films they want us to view, and listening to the music they want us to listen to. It might be possible to manipulate someone's brain to be the sort of brain we want it to be, but that demands far more from behavioural pressures than from genetic ones. This is a reminder that an individual's uniqueness is placed in jeopardy by forcing them to perform in a preordained manner (Jones, 2002b).

Clones would have a different sense of self, different thought processes, and different ethical responsibility. Their uniqueness as persons would remain intact, because they would be true individuals. Of course, there would be some overlap with an individual who had already existed (and might still exist), but this is hardly unique. All of us overlap genetically with our biological parents. The degree of overlap would be greater with clones than with the rest of us, but if provided with an open future by their families their originality as people would be intact. There is also no reason why they would not also demonstrate spiritual uniqueness. From a Christian perspective, the value of human beings rests on a dignity bestowed by God and is independent of genetic or social status. Theologically, personhood and identity are God's gracious gift, and not something that humans can manufacture or copy.

Anyone hoping that the production of a human clone

would replicate or replace a previously existing person would be sadly let down (compare JOHN DOBBS and john dobbs (M)). This is another way of stating that the design element in reproductive cloning is extremely rudimentary. Any fears one might have regarding human reproductive cloning should not be grounded in the power of designing babies or adults. Cloning has little future in this regard.

Genetic design and personal characteristics

While it is relatively easy to dismiss the extremes surrounding reproductive cloning, the realm of genetic control is a far subtler one. It is in this context that reference is repeatedly made to gay genes, IQ genes, and genes for aggression. In the media one even reads of God genes and infidelity genes! Regardless of which gene one is allegedly interested in, the basic message is the same – there are genes that cause us to act in certain ways. The underlying assumption is that there is a direct correlation between genes and disease, genes and behaviour, and even genes and belief. The alluring possibility is that it might even be on the cards that we can choose the genes we want for our children: an intelligent one, a beautiful one, and a virtuous one. But what about producing one who is all three – intelligent, beautiful and virtuous?

No wonder many despair at the direction being taken by genetics. The debate so often seems to revolve around producing individuals who are compliant with our wishes; they can become entrepreneurs, scientists, or accountants, whatever we wish. Or they will excel at chess, football or ballet. For those with religious leanings, it might prove possible to genetically engineer them so as to increase the likelihood that our offspring follow Christ. Take your pick; all that is required is choice of the appropriate genes!

These are disturbing possibilities, since they undermine central elements within our responsibility as human beings. If I have no choice but to be aggressive, I might find myself unable to follow Christ's injunction to be a peacemaker and to love my neighbour as myself. It might even be that the fruits of the Spirit cannot manifest themselves in my life, not because I am being unfaithful, but because I am genetically inclined to be jealous, angry and selfish. Could my Christian journey amount to nothing more than a genetic predisposition?

These are unsettling vistas, because they presuppose that all we stand for can be explained in genetic terms, which is usually interpreted as explaining away everything we stand for. We live according to certain basic genetic designs; modify the designs, and we become different people with different personal characteristics. Look to the future and individuals will be designed according to some controllers' whims. All is in the genes and the genes explain everything. But is this the case?

The link between individual genes and behaviour is far more complex than suggested by the "gene for X" scenario. This is because multiple interacting genetic factors usually contribute to a trait. Besides this, environmental factors are also of major relevance, interacting with genetic factors in a complex manner. Interestingly, genes are switched on and off in response to a variety of pressures, both during development and later on in cell life, while the proteins produced by genes may subsequently be modified themselves (Nuffield Council on Bioethics, 2002).

Consequently, the actions of a single gene (or even a set of genes) will rarely be the only cause of a particular condition. The pathway between a gene, a particular protein, and an individual scoring highly on an IQ test, or having an aggressive personality, is very indirect. Genes influence behaviour, but concentrating on genes to the exclusion of all other factors grossly oversimplifies the human condition.

The world of behavioural genetics points clearly to the conclusion that aspects of our character and personal identity have a genetic basis. This is not surprising, as there is an intimate link between what we are as persons and the bodies we possess as embodied persons. Genetic factors are inevitably involved, even at the deepest levels of what makes us the people we are. But this in no way threatens the conception of a person as a rational being, capable of taking responsibility for him- or herself as a free agent. Neither does it detract from our ability to act as God's agents and stewards in his created order (Jones, 2004a).

The freedom of human beings is not an absolute one. We cannot do anything we like on a purely biological level, let alone morally. Our freedom is a limited freedom, since we always operate within boundaries imposed by biological and environmental circumstances, including our genetic make-up. This is why so much of the discussion of the potential and problems of genetics is unhelpful, giving as it does the impression that one day all limits will be swept away and human powers will become limitless. They will have achieved Godlike status, able to design as they please, and create anything that enters their imaginations. Such fantasies should be summarily dismissed. On the other hand, an appreciation of the limited nature of what we can do as human beings is valuable, because it helps us appreciate our moral and spiritual limits, as well as our addictions and predispositions. We can also learn how God's grace can renew what we are as people, working through our physical bodies and genetic substratum.

We are "of the earth", and we recognise that God himself was incarnated to become one with us: to become flesh (John 1:1–14), with (among many other things) its genetic building blocks. These building blocks, however, are far from unalterable, since the environment affects everything to which they give rise. Surprisingly, this includes the micro-environment at the level of cells and tissues, as well as the far more obvious external influences. Hence, it is unwise to attempt to see genes as isolated units. The relationship between genes and a diversity of environmental influences is an intimately interlocked one.

What this means is that genes are influenced indirectly as well as directly. Advertently or inadvertently, their expression may be modified by the nature of the environment in which children grow up and function. People and their bodies do not exist in a social vacuum. A vast range of genetic and social factors will always exist alongside one another.

Compare the quality of life of the following: i) those with potentially excellent health but who are living in a malnourished community where their efforts are devoted to mere survival; ii) those brought up in abusive homes and characterised by behavioural problems as adults; iii) those with cystic fibrosis or some other equally debilitating condition but who are brought up in loving and supportive homes and communities; and iv) in the future, those brought into the world by cloning or following genetic modification of some description but who are raised in a loving environment where they are cherished for all they represent as individuals in their own right (Jones, 2002b).

Here we have different forms of control – *social* in the first two and *biological* in the latter two. None of these outcomes is inevitable, regardless of the genetic influences. What is of crucial significance is the ability to be oneself and to relate productively to others within the human community. Relationships such as these emanate from our personhood, as those made in the image of a triune God. The manner in which humans are treated should always be viewed within the broader context provided by human relationships, and never simply within the much narrower framework of biological parameters. Any choices we make should be choices to benefit people, and not simply to enhance disconnected building blocks, whether genes, livers or brains.

This is the essence of a person-centred model. We make choices for ourselves and on behalf of others, because people have to make choices. Some of these choices will not raise any genetic or technological issues, and do not generally elicit vigorous ethical debate. Others will, such as when genetic choices are made at the earliest stages of children's existence – probably when they are or were embryos. The thrust of my argument is that non-genetic and genetic choices should be viewed within a unitary framework.

What then has become of design, which as we have seen will always be limited in extent? Any assessment of its ethical or theological validity will depend upon the considerations we have already encountered.

- What is it aiming to achieve?
- Is the aim realistic or is it an illustration of bravado?
- How safe is it?
- Will the future individual's life be enhanced in some important fashion?
- Will the individual's possibility of relating to God be heightened?
- Will the individual's ability to contribute constructively to the human community be improved?
- What impact will it have on society and on the character of society?

From hubris to humility

This discussion has pointed to a place for design within genetics, but design of a far more limited and humble variety than so often encountered in these debates. It is far removed from the bravado and hubris associated with the picture of a factory production line of identical and preordained babies. The challenge is to determine how we do these things, and under what circumstances we do them, because this is where responsibility, judgement and discernment come into play. We can't do anything we like; we shouldn't *attempt* to do anything we like. But we should do all we can to improve the quality of the lives of those around us, whether by using biological means or simply by treating them as beings of importance and as people who matter.

This, it seems to me, is where Christians should be contributing to this debate. If we consider that God is concerned with the world he has made, his concern will extend to the genetic realm, just as it does to every other aspect of human life, human community, and the non-human biological and physical world. Divine grace and creativity are evident in all these realms, and human creativity is to follow suit. If we can say that God works through creation and, therefore, through what we describe as the natural world, there is no reason to say that he does not also work through the basic processes described by biology and, therefore, through genetic mechanisms. If this is true, we can go on to say that genetic modification brought about by humans – genetic design if you like – has the potential for extending the work of God. Of course, this has enormous dangers and pitfalls, since appallingly injudicious choices can be made, but this is also true of every other area of human life.

Nevertheless, it is at this point that I part company with

some other Christians, who stress what they view as the almost inevitable problems with genetic technology. Their responses are mired in deep concerns, which dominate every facet of their attitudes towards genetics. Consider the following statement by Nancy L. Jones and John F. Kilner (2004):

> The genetics and genomics revolution has at its core information and techniques that can be used to change humanness itself as well as the concepts of what it means to be human. The age-old human fantasies of the mythical chimeras of the ancients, supernatural intelligence, wiping disease from human inheritance, designing a better human being, the fountain of youth, and even immortality now have biotechnical credence in the theoretical promises of genetics and genetic engineering. Not only can humanity's collective genetic inheritance be shaped by selecting which embryos are allowed to develop via pre-implantation genetic diagnosis, but genetic engineering, the availability of the human embryo for experimentation, and combining genes from many species require only sufficient imagination to catalyze the designing of a new humanity.

The assumption underlying a statement of this nature is that hubris will dominate. Consequently, the Christian response is to oppose what is viewed as an inevitable road to destruction. While I cannot be totally assured that such an end will not eventuate, I also cling to what I view as God's oversight of the world he has created. For me, the Christian response is to approach these and similar technologies with humility, which I regard as essential for rigorously assessing the merits of what can and cannot be accomplished by genetic science. Using the therapeutic and person-centred framework I am advocating, our eyes can be directed towards what can realistically be accomplished to benefit the patient. This is a far cry from the hubris sometimes encountered, but also from the anti-hubris that has become so caught up in the fear of extravagant claims that it has lost sight of the good that could be accomplished by utilising some of these technologies.

But is my stress on humility unattainable? Is it a Christian ideal that will for ever be quenched, overpowered by agendas based on commercial gain, political pre-eminence and simple self-centredness? I have to admit these are all possibilities, even (some would say) probabilities. No technological advances bring unalloyed good; that which will benefit mankind seems to be inextricably interwoven with the interests of the powerful and the destructive. And there appears to be no way of isolating the one from the other. I accept this, since I come from a Christian tradition that acknowledges the sinfulness of the human race as well as its grandeur; its depravity alongside its glory. And so when considering questions of design, I cannot deny that some will wish to direct the emerging technologies towards the production of elite athletes rather than, or as well as, towards alleviating the horrors of AD or schizophrenia or AIDS. However, I do not accept that this leads to the inevitable conclusion that we walk away from contemplating any possibilities in these areas, or even that we devote ourselves to attempting to ban all genetic ventures. What are required are realism and regulation, as we attempt to obtain the best from what are always uncertain undertakings.

Inevitably, there is a cautionary lesson here, and this is to beware of obsession with the normal, something that could be accentuated by any of the current biomedical technologies. The genetic realm is as limited as any other, and talk of designing wonderful new human beings is futile. On the other hand, the rejection of a modicum of limited and very cautious design is the outcome of a spirit of fear rather than of a spirit of faithfulness. We are to do what is consistent with the nature and purposes of God, and should assess all scientific developments by the benchmark of whether they appear to forward God's work in creation. Daunting as these tasks are, and inadequate as we are to tackle them, they are enriched when theological, scientific and ethical insights are brought to bear on them in an integrated fashion.

Chapter 3

What is Special About the Human Embryo?

For some readers, the previous chapters will have failed to come to terms with an underlying issue that should have appeared right at the start, and this is the status of the human embryo. For many, this is the beginning and end of all discussion on issues and procedures at the beginning of human life. This has to be sorted out before anything else can be discussed. However, I have problems with this, and I deliberately did not set out my discussion in this way, because in my view it is important to map out the context of the discussion first. It is also very obvious that discussion frequently stalls at this first hurdle, making it impossible to proceed any further in a productive manner.

We live in a world where there is no agreement on the status of the human embryo. This applies across societies; it also applies within Christian circles. It is hopeless, therefore, to get bogged down in any one view of the human embryo, to the exclusion of all others, and also to view the human embryo as the only object of concern. Discussions of the legitimacy of war do not begin and end with the status of human life. This is assumed. Even those who in other contexts argue that all human life is sacred will generally allow killing in war under certain circumstances. The same applies with even greater force to discussions at the commencement of human life, since there is no general agreement on embryonic status, no matter how strongly some feel about the rightness of their own position.

From simplicity to perplexity

A short time ago, when visiting a church in England, I picked up a leaflet advertising a series of meetings hosted by a Christian organisation established to demonstrate the manner in which the Christian faith should be addressing questions of relevance for contemporary society (The Christian Institute, 2003). In outlining what the organisation stood for, the leaflet informed its readers that one of its fundamental tenets is that "human life is sacred from conception". This statement is interesting for a number of reasons. The first is that it is regarded by this organisation as foundational for Christian witness in modern society; it appears to be non-negotiable, and one assumes that without it Christian witness will be muted. The second is the assurance with which it is propounded; it is true, and by definition any position deviating from it will not be true. We are not told on what grounds it is true, or whether these have been derived from biblical teaching, theological reflection, church tradition, contemporary Western science, ethics, philosophy or experience. The third is what the statement actually conveys: the sacredness of human life, and its sacredness from its very first glimmerings. One assumes from this that human life is sacred in a way in which all non-human life is not sacred. But what does the claim for sacredness actually mean? Are we sacred (holy, sacrosanct) in a way in which God is sacred, or is there a difference?

A statement like this causes me immense problems, which I touched on briefly in Chapter 1, and yet many Christians will be very happy with it. They will see it as a bulwark of the Christian faith, and will readily agree with this organisation in setting it forth in such categorical terms. For many, it is indeed foundational, since it alone will keep in check the rampant runaway forces of modern science and in particular the potentially dehumanising reproductive technologies. We are living on a battlefield with the might of atheistic science arrayed against the armies of Christ. Since the first is intent on destroying all that is worthy and uplifting, the second should be devoted to attempting to conserve all that is truly human. This is a battle for the future of humankind, and the sacredness of human life from conception is the supreme weapon we possess.

It is no exaggeration to state that many conservative Christians accept the sacredness–conception duality as a basic dogma without which all is lost (Hui, 2002). Its non-negotiable nature is self-evident, and it readily becomes a mark of faithfulness to the gospel of Christ. And so, when confronted by the reproductive technologies, it is sometimes argued that the truly Christian response is to question whether we utilise them at all, because once that is allowed we have relinquished our moral and spiritual authority.

There may be a place for dogma, but before anything is elevated to this level of assent, enormous care is required to ensure that its truthfulness is completely assured. It also needs to be assented to by a broad range of interested people; in this instance by a broad range of theologians, philosophers, scientists and ethicists from within the Christian community. This is because, if it fails to gain such acceptance, it will prove divisive rather than foundational; it will destroy rather than build up. Such comments are appropriate in this instance. The truthfulness of the sacredness–conception duality is critical, because if it is wrong, or even if it is simply misleading, the end result will be a marginalising of Christians as they get caught on the wrong side of a science–faith battle (Jones, 2004b).

It is not my intention to analyse the sacredness–conception duality in a direct manner in this chapter. Rather, I intend to raise doubts, by introducing yet further questions and queries. The reproductive area is a deeply perplexing one for everybody, but perhaps especially so for those working within a Christian framework. While, as we have just seen, some Christians have no doubts, others are far from convinced, especially when confronted by some of the dilemmas encountered in real life. No matter what position we adopt on issues at the beginning of human life, we should be struck by the difficulty and perplexity of this whole area.

When does human life begin?

The question generally in people's minds is: when does human life begin? To this apparently simple question, many people want an equally simple answer. It is at point X or point Y. Before point X there is nothing; after point X there is everything. Or, alternatively, before point Y there is nothing of great moral concern; after point Y there is something of inestimable value. The pressure to give such an answer is usually immense; so much so that people feel aggrieved when they are not provided with one, even if it is an answer with which they can take issue. To refuse to answer such a simple question is seen as obfuscating, as being pig-headed, or as the sad indecision of an impoverished thinker. There *must* be an answer to such an age-old question. Surely anyone in the business of ethics or moral theology has had time to formulate their position, which by definition will indicate a clear point of demarcation? And for scores of Christians the *correct* answer is conception.

However, I refuse to capitulate this easily. When people ask: "When does human life begin?", what sort of answer do they expect? Are they looking for an answer that is scientific, philosophical, theological, social, or a mixture of all four? As we think about this question, we should also ask ourselves why we are interested in it and in the answer that may emerge. What issues will an answer help us resolve? How might an answer to this basic question affect the way in which we value, and therefore treat, embryonic and fetal humans? Might it have ramifications for the manner in which we treat children and adults?

Abortion has been the traditional reason behind asking (and I presume answering) this question, and ethical discussions on the reproductive technologies continue to be dominated by abortion. But there is a snag here, since the emphasis in abortion is on the late embryo and fetus (from seven to eight weeks onwards), whereas bioethical discussions on reproductive issues focus on the early embryo, in particular on the pre-implantation embryo (up to fourteen days post-fertilisation). These differences in timing may be of profound ethical (and even theological) significance, a significance that is completely missed if the discussion commences with the parameters set by abortion. Neither is this of mere theoretical interest, since human embryos have been available for study in the laboratory for over 30 years. As soon as this became feasible, they could be assessed for abnormalities, and they could be used for research purposes. All these occur in connection with IVF and with studies on the causes of infertility and diseases afflicting embryos. More recently, they have taken us into the realm of stem-cell technology, and of somatic cell nuclear transfer (SCNT; therapeutic and research cloning).

In other words, what has become paramount is the status of the very early human embryo, especially the blastocyst (a fluid-filled entity at five to seven days into development [post-fertilisation]). These blastocysts contain an inner cell mass (ICM), some of the cells of which will ultimately give rise to the new individual, and external trophectoderm cells, which give rise to the future placenta and support tissues (see below). The status of blastocysts is central to ethical debate, since they are capable of serving as a source of stem cells, which may eventually play a crucial role in producing new cell lines for the repair of adult tissues. However, there is an additional ethical issue that has not featured prominently in ethical or theological debate, and this is whether there is any difference in status between the blastocysts in a woman's uterus and the blastocysts in a laboratory, that is, between *in vivo* (*in utero*) and *in vitro* blastocysts respectively. Might there be a differential value between these two groups of blastocysts, on the grounds that the prospects of developing into a new individual are present in the first group but absent in the second? And how are they to be valued in comparison with children and adults? The way in which one answers these questions will determine the lengths to which one is prepared to go to protect blastocysts.

Although I shall be discussing blastocysts, very recent research has shown that stem cells can be obtained from an even earlier stage in embryonic development – the morula, at around three days after fertilisation.

What are we talking about?

When we ask the question "When does human life begin?", what are we asking? Are we talking about a new human existence, in the sense in which a new *biological* unit has come into play? In other words, is it the same as asking when does a new dog life begin for a dog or a new rat life for a rat? At the purely biological level, it is self-evident that a new human life begins once the process of fertilisation has been completed, simply because that is the start of a whole host of processes that, given a supportive environment and in a minority of instances, will end in an adult organism, whether this be human, dog or rat. Even this, taken in isolation from any other considerations, does not provide a very precise answer, because fertilisation itself is a process incorporating a series of important steps. Of course, even here there is a potential trap; development may not commence with fertilisation but with SCNT. Cloning will force a restatement of this biological position if and when human cloning enters the picture. However, there is no doubt that what one is dealing with from one to two days onwards is human tissue, and like all other human tissue this is to be treated with a degree of moral circumspection beyond that appropriate for non-human tissue.

But is a biological answer the one most people are interested in? To this question there is a wide variety of answers, because what people are generally concerned with is how much *value* or *protection* should be bestowed on an embryo. This is the reason why a distinction between human life and personhood is frequently introduced, a distinction between "*being human*" (as with the biological definition) and "*being a person*" (when the biological entity should be valued as a human person). What this distinction signifies is that, with the recognition of personhood, an individual must be valued and protected exactly as all human persons are valued and protected. By implication, there may be those who are human, but who are not persons in the fullest sense, and therefore do not have the protection we normally expect to give to persons. Possibly early embryos fit into this category, especially early embryos in the laboratory.

When expressed like this, it is not surprising that this distinction horrifies some people on the ground that no human beings should ever be classed as non-persons. For some, not even a newly fertilised egg, let alone a human blastocyst, can be classed as a non-person. All are persons simply because they are human; no additional criteria are necessary. This is the position of many conservative Christians. For them the distinction between humans as biological entities and humans as persons devalues human life, since a newly fertilised egg and a blastocyst are as morally significant as any of us reading this book. They also fear that this distinction might lead to a situation whereby fetuses, the mentally retarded and the demented are also demoted to a non-personal status and are regarded as disposable.

Some Christians also make the *theological* point that, since all humans are made in the image and likeness of God, one cannot conclude that any humans are worth less than any other humans (Hui, 2002). Hence, since the earliest of human embryos are made in God's image, they must be given total protection. If God loves them, so must we; hence, under no circumstances should research be conducted on any human embryos unless it is for the benefit of those particular embryos. To claim to love an embryo, but then carry out destructive research on it, is seen as a contradiction in terms. In arguing like this, they are placing the earliest of embryos on precisely the same footing as every other human being on the basis of God's love for them. They are full members of the human community.

As with every issue in this early developmental area, these theological statements raise queries of their own. How do we know that God loves every embryo, and what does God's love for blastocysts actually mean? Did Christ die for every blastocyst, including those innumerable blastocysts that are biologically incapable of developing beyond two to three weeks' gestation because of built-in abnormalities? And, if so, what does that mean and how do we know? Similarly, what does the image of God mean in the case of blastocysts, both those capable of developing further and those incapable of doing so?

On the surface, these questions give the appearance of being worthlessly erudite and far removed from everyday reality. And yet, when confronted by decisions about conducting research on human embryos, answers have to be given to such questions, if it is thought that the questions themselves are relevant. And, for some people, the answers might be shocking, since one could conclude that blastocysts as a whole, or certain groups of blastocysts, are not the specific objects of God's love and are not made in God's image. This is a daily concern for those working in fertility clinics, where decisions are being made about which embryos to implant in a woman undergoing IVF, those considered to be viable and those considered non-viable. If both groups are regarded as imaging God, is there a moral and spiritual obligation to implant non-viable as well as viable embryos, on the ground that this obligation entails doing everything possible to actualise the potential for life even when the possibility of success is remote?

Alternative approaches

Although my emphasis has been on either/or perspectives, there are alternative positions that view embryos and fetuses as increasing in status and worth as biological and personal development unfolds, and perhaps also growing into the image of God. Such positions attempt to take seriously biological phenomena that characterise the growing embryo, including the emergence of well-defined organisation and individuality, alongside a decrease in the potential of its cells to be redirected (Jones 1987, 2000a). There is a sense of a "coming into being" along the continuum that marks embryonic development.

But what are we dealing with scientifically? The fertilised egg is a single cell, the zygote, and is totipotent, giving rise eventually to the fetus and placenta. This single cell undergoes cleavage, during which it divides with little intervening growth to produce two, then four, then eight smaller, identical cells. These are the blastomeres, which at the eight-cell stage are only loosely associated with one another, and have the potential to develop into complete adults if separated from the remaining blastomeres. By the 32-cell stage, they have become increasingly adherent and closely packed, and have almost definitely lost this equal developmental potential.

As the number of cells continues to increase, those on the outside of the group become firmly attached to one another, with the internal ones remaining unconnected. This stage, at around five to seven days, is the blastocyst. The outer cells are in the process of differentiating and forming a surface layer, the trophectoderm, which becomes the trophoblast when implantation occurs in the wall of the mother's uterus (completed by fourteen days). These trophoblastic cells eventually give rise to the placenta. By contrast, the inner cells constituting the inner cell mass (ICM) are still undifferentiated, and it is from a small number of these cells that the future individual arises.

By fourteen days after fertilisation, a structure known as the embryonic disc develops, and it is this that becomes the embryo proper. At fifteen to sixteen days a few thousand cells in the disc migrate to the midline, where they form the primitive streak, which is a transitory developmental structure. This instigates the appearance of the neural plate, from which arises the first rudiment of the nervous system early in the third week of gestation. By about 28 days, the beginnings of the central nervous system are present, although individual parts of the brain are not recognisable until five to six weeks' gestation.

The primitive streak has assumed a position of major importance in ethical debate. Its appearance at around fifteen to sixteen days has been widely regarded as marking a point of transition, with some arguing that no coherent entity exists prior to this, so that it is misleading to refer to anything earlier as a human individual. Conversely, commitment to developing into an individual embryo is present by the primitive streak stage, from which point onwards a spatially defined entity capable of developing into a fetus and infant begins to exist. While these points are made within a scientific framework, they send out powerful ethical and regulatory messages, so that in those societies where research on human embryos is permitted the dominance of the fourteen-day upper limit to research is currently unchallenged.

In view of these findings it will come as no surprise to learn that, for many writers coming from quite different religious traditions and scientific perspectives, the alternative to conception is fourteen days. This is based on many well known arguments regarding the completion of implantation, the appearance of the primitive streak (followed by indications of the earliest hint of a nervous system), the impossibility of twinning, and the presence of a far higher percentage of cells committed to forming the embryo proper (e.g. Ford, 1988; Shannon & Walter 2003; Peters 2003b; Bryant & Searle 2004). I have considerable sympathy with this position, although I do not want it to be regarded as a line in the sand. Admittedly, there have to be clear legal definitions, and this one is as good as any in practice at the present time. Nevertheless, even this should not constrain us in our thinking, and push us into arguing for the lack of any meaningful human life at thirteen days but the presence of such life at fifteen days. The unfolding of a developing organism does not lend itself to such precision, while the value we ascribe to a developing organism does not change this rapidly. As a result, in both scientific and theological terms, I remain agnostic on a definitive point. I do not believe we should search for one, or pretend we have found one.

The presence of cells in the five-to-seven-day-old blastocyst that contribute directly to the future individual should make us hesitate to set too much store by a fourteen-day line in the sand. Additionally, it is unwise to regard the blastocyst or embryo in isolation from all other factors as though these are self-existing and self-generating entities. They are not, although little in ethical or theological debate provides even a hint that this is the case.

Environmental and community considerations

One of the characteristics of the debate on the status of early embryos has been that they are usually viewed, as I have just noted, as isolated and essentially self-contained entities. Their status, whatever it may be, is inherent to them. They have this status regardless of where they are encountered – in a woman's uterine tubes, in a woman's uterus embedded in the uterine wall, in a woman's abdominal cavity (as in an ectopic pregnancy), in a Petri dish in the laboratory, or in a laboratory freezer. For some they are human persons in all these locations, even though they lack the potential to become fully developed persons in a number of them. In other words, this perspective takes no account of the embryo's environment. Neither does it take any account of the human community within which the embryos are encountered.

Human embryos never exist in isolation from others,

even in the laboratory, and it can be argued that they should always be viewed within the context of the human community. Their existence and flourishing are dependent upon others within this community and on the relationships they have with others. This observation elicits two responses. Since they are the weakest of all human forms, they should be protected under all circumstances. Their dependence on other human beings is the crucial ethical and theological driver, leading to opposition to their use in any research or therapeutic projects. An alternative response is to assess the worth of very early embryos alongside that of other human beings. It is a comparative worth. But once the claim of comparative, as opposed to absolute, worth is made, the whole tenor of ethical and theological discussion changes. This is because the relationships within the human community are brought to the fore, and the spotlight is directed onto human decision-making, responsibility and control. How does this affect the embryo's standing as one who, potentially at least, is in the image of God? Is it demoted or enhanced?

Any attempt to answer these questions has to resort to the environmental paradigm. Blastocysts are found naturally, as well as artificially, in a range of environments, some of which enhance their ontogenetic development, whereas others hinder it. In other words, some blastocysts possess the inherent, as well as the environmental, potential to become flourishing individuals; others lack this potential on one or other score. While this is a biological observation, it introduces theological considerations. Does talk about the image of God also involve environmental considerations, in that it refers to "blastocyst + conducive environment" rather than "blastocyst" alone (Towns & Jones, 2004a)? If it refers equally to both groups, the implication is that a blastocyst with no potential for further development still images God. This amounts to an argument in favour of all human tissue being in the image of God; that is, as isolated human tissue rather than as tissue integral to a human person.

What, then, about *conflict situations*, the best known of which is the one between fetus and pregnant woman in abortion dilemmas? Such situations are, however, not confined to the well-worn topic of abortion. They are becoming common features of the reproductive area: for instance, the choice between disposing of an embryo or fetus, or using it for research or therapeutic purposes. Following induced abortion, disposal of the remains is the usual course of action. But what if some of this tissue can be used to assist a patient in need? Should this ever be contemplated, or is it almost by definition unethical and a mark of disrespect for the recently killed fetus? Regardless of the decision we reach, there is conflict here: between using tissue from a dead fetus for a good purpose, and automatically disposing of the tissue on the grounds that this alone shows respect for a dead fetus (Jones, 1991). The equivalent situation for embryos is the conflict between obtaining stem cells from an early embryo surplus to the requirements of a couple in an IVF programme and routinely disposing of that embryo. Which is the better path? The frequently encountered response in Christian circles is that surplus embryos should never be produced, thus bypassing the conflict. While this represents one particular ideal, numerous surplus embryos exist in most countries. What is to be done with these embryos, since they cannot be ignored? They will not disappear. How can the sacredness–conception duality respond to this dilemma?

These are exceedingly demanding and tantalising questions, the newness of which adds to their problematic nature. It is appropriate, therefore, to ask whether there are any special perspectives that Christians might bring to the debate.

Are there theological perspectives that will provide specific insights unattainable by any other route?

Searching for biblical themes

There is no way in which the biblical writers could give specific answers to the type of questions considered here (Alexander & White, 2004). The Bible does not specifically map out the significance of fertilisation any more than it maps out the significance of blastocysts in the laboratory. Nevertheless, there are general principles that stem in large part from the incarnation, when Jesus revealed the image of God in human form and thereby demonstrated the importance of bodily existence. These principles help lay the groundwork for our thinking about human beings. These are that human beings:

- are created in God's image;
- are precious to God;
- have a special status;
- are to be treated with dignity because this stems from God's love and concern for them;
- are to be respected.

As general as these themes are, they are foundational, constituting important guideposts for all our thinking about the ways in which human beings are to be treated. These themes impart to all humans a splendour and significance that we dare not overlook, whether this be in reproductive ethics, numerous aspects of social policy, or international relations. They point *towards* equality, compassion and protection, and *away from* inequality, exploitation and social programming. But where does this leave life before birth? References to pre-natal human existence are encountered in passages such as

Job 10:3–12, Psalm 139:13–16, Isaiah 49:1, Jeremiah 1:5, and Luke 1:41–44, where pre-natal humans emerge as part of the human community, and therefore are to be viewed as special to us and to God (Jones, 1999).

The points that emerge are well known, and have been worked through repeatedly. Nevertheless, despite their general nature, they bear reiterating:

- There is continuity between life before and life after birth. The one leads on to the other and may influence the other. Obvious as this observation may be, it helps to direct our thinking by reminding us that the biblical writers did not envisage some huge chasm between life before and life after birth. They did not see birth as the start of the individual's human journey. There was something important before birth, and this was recognised and taken into account in their thinking.

- As God's servants, such as David and Jeremiah, looked back at God's concern for them throughout their lives, they recognised that God had known them and cared for them before as well as after birth. They were aware that the individuals they were in adult life had some indissoluble continuity with what they had been before birth (Psalm 22:9,10; 139:13; Jeremiah 1:5). The God whom they experienced as being faithful in the present had also been faithful throughout the whole of their earthly histories. David and Jeremiah were exulting in the realisation that God had been with them from the earliest stages of their existence, a realisation that carried immense spiritual weight.

- The spiritual nature of this relationship with God becomes even more evident when David and Jeremiah discern that the one who was looking after them in the present had in some mysterious way looked after them from eternity. God "beheld" David long before he was formed in the womb (Psalm 139:15,16); God "knew" Jeremiah and consecrated him as a prophet long before Jeremiah's body took on the form of a human being (Jeremiah 1:5). These are powerful theological statements, according to which their pre-natal existence (before and after conception) was seen as God's work, expressing his purposes, and directed towards his glory.

- Human life is a gift of God (Genesis 4:1; 16:2; 29:31,32; 30:22,23; Ruth 4:13). It is viewed as an act of creation in which both humans and God have their essential roles to play. It is the gift of new life to the one who has come into existence and who can reflect on his past, a gift that springs from human decision-making and actions, both responsible and irresponsible.

These are crucial points for a Christian perspective, forming as they do the bedrock of much Christian thinking on God's provisions for his people at all stages of their human lives. His interest does not commence at birth, but neither does it commence at fertilisation. It has dimensions that transcend human existence, and take us into the eternal purposes of God. Consequently, a biological interpretation of these passages will let us down badly, no matter how worthy our intentions.

From this it follows that it would be unwise to jump too rapidly from passages like these into the midst of contemporary reproductive issues. The worlds and the interests are quite different. These passages reveal the testimonies of a very small number of people about the ways in which God had led them and looked after them. They are personal and private confessions about God and his purposes for them. They are far removed from the aseptic clinical world of reproductive technologies or the equally aseptic world of academic discussions on the moral status of embryos and fetuses. The closest we come to this today are individuals testifying to God's dealings with them throughout their lives – exact parallels to some of these Old Testament confessions. But they also contain elements we find very difficult, or perhaps impossible, to understand. How could God care for them as non-existent beings, way back in his time – if we can call it time – and not in our time? What we have here is a mystery, perhaps a profound mystery, and possibly of immense importance for faith, but surely of little relevance to ethical issues about how embryos are to be treated.

These biblical passages touching on pre-natal life are confessions about God and his purposes, and are not designed to impart information about the precise status of embryonic life. Their context is always that of living people looking back on the way in which God had looked after them since their earliest beginnings, and about God's purposes for them from eternity. God's purposes are always central; any biology or ethical directives we may glean from these passages is incidental.

Can we move from personal expressions of praise by God's people for his faithfulness to them before birth to an understanding of how God views *all* embryos and fetuses? This represents a seismic shift from the particular to the general, from confessions about God's activities in the lives of *particular* individuals to statements about how *everyone* should view embryos *en masse*. This is where different perspectives emerge among Christians. Any move from the particular to the general in any direct sense involves making vast conceptual leaps for which I can find no biblical warrant. God's protection of David's embryo does not justify the assertion that he expects contemporary societies to protect every embryo brought into existence. If the latter is the case, it has to be argued on other grounds.

The furthest I consider we can go is to state that God is concerned about embryos and fetuses, just as he is concerned about human life after birth. This is where the general principles of special status, dignity and respect enter the picture. What this leads to is a serious commitment to the welfare of embryos and fetuses. This ensures that we never treat human life before birth frivolously and that we never underestimate the worth of those who may be like us in the future. In very general terms, the population of embryos is an important population, just as is the post-natal population. They might not be of equal importance, but there is at least partial equivalence and there are interrelationships we dare not overlook. We are, therefore, to extend neighbour love to pre-natal human life (Peterson, 2001) and are to value pre-natal life (Meilaender, 1996).

One of the striking features of the biblical writings is that they leave a great deal unsaid that would have been of interest to us today. Passages such as the ones I have mentioned provide few clues about the significance of determining precisely when human life begins, since the biblical writers did not think in these terms, and they did not address the question of whether a very early embryo is a person with the rights of a person. The writers were not interested in questions like these, and, even if they had been, they did not possess the tools to formulate concepts that are routinely accepted today. What emerges from this is that problems like the treatment of blastocysts are *our* problems, and it is *our* responsibility to decide what response is appropriate for those seeking to be faithful to God. We will not find ready-made answers in Scripture. The place of the Bible in different Christian approaches to contemporary biomedical issues is discussed in Chapter 4.

We have obligations to take as seriously as we can the dignity of embryos and fetuses, alongside the dignity of all others within the human community. Inevitably, there will be conflicts and possibly compromises. Where do we start?

Making decisions about embryos

The problem of working prospectively

The biblical passages about David and Jeremiah suggest that we can work retrospectively (see also Chapter 4). Looking back, we can make certain statements about God's care and protection of us. Steve may well be able to say that God has looked after Steve French throughout his life, from fertilisation onwards, including those times when he was very ill as a two-year-old and following a serious car accident when he was eighteen. He knows that God loves him deeply. But can Steve have the same assurance of God's relationship with the two embryos that they suspect (but are not sure) his wife lost? They are delighted with the two growing children they do have, and they see God's hand protecting them at various testing times.

But can we move prospectively? We know that it is impossible to protect *all* early embryos, since vast numbers are lost naturally. But can we say that *this* early embryo (E) is to be protected as opposed to *that* early embryo (F)? This question has little relevance during normal pregnancy, except when decisions are being made about abortion, and then it is dealing with fetuses. However, it is relevant when dealing with early embryos in a laboratory situation, where decisions have to be made between embryos on the basis of their viability, or on whether they are or are not carrying particular deleterious genes. As the focus falls onto these specific embryos (embryo E as opposed to embryo F), can we say that the knowledge and care of God apply to some of these (E, let us say) but not to others, like F? Do we possess theological insights on specific blastocysts?

As far as I can see, the answer to this question must be "no". Even those who contend that every blastocyst must be preserved have no inside knowledge on each one. Their position is governed by a belief that all human life is sacred and must be preserved, and hence is a commitment to conserve the whole of the embryonic population. This position does not enable choices to be made between blastocysts in a clinical situation, where responsible human decision-making demands choices.

But what if blastocysts are a gift of God? If they represent the gift of new life, and if choices are made between them, only some blastocysts will experience this gift. This is true, but this also applies routinely in natural fertilisation and development, where many embryos are lost. This suggests that to equate each blastocyst with a new human life and gift of God is premature. We simply do not know at this early stage of development whether a meaningful new human life has come into existence. Human tissue is present, but is a blastocyst more than this, especially when *in vitro* blastocysts still have to be placed in a woman's uterus to mature into human individuals?

This line of questioning is in accordance with those writers who regard a point at around fourteen days or so as a biologically and theologically significant transition into a discernible new human life (Ford, 1988; Shannon & Walter, 2003). For instance, Shannon and Walter (2003) are adamant that one cannot speak of an individual for up to three weeks into development, until individualisation has occurred. Before that time, they claim, the pre-implantation embryo represents what is common to humanity. They write (p. 128):

> The genetic structure [of the pre-implantation embryo] is generic to the species but is not yet identified with a particular individual ... we do not have an ontological individual.

In the light of this, these writers consider that pre-implantation embryos have a pre-moral value in that they are living, bear the human genome, and have a teleology directed to the moral category of personhood (Shannon & Walter, 2003, p. 130). A fuller discussion of this appears in Chapter 4, along with an outline of the emphasis that Peters (2003b) lays on dignity, which for him is first conferred and then claimed. Having been conferred by God, it is we who confer it on one another, including on embryos. Dignity, then, has two features: it depends ultimately on God's love, and it is relational in character. Hence, to confer dignity on an embryo is a gesture of hope about/for what it will ultimately become, rather than a seeking after the significance of its genetic origin. On this basis, Peters recognises the centrality of choice in deciding what courses of action are appropriate regarding what should or should not be done to pre-implantation embryos.

Manipulating embryos

Does this suggest that we can do anything we like with early embryos? I suggest that we cannot, since it is the nature of the decision-making that is crucial. The choices I envisage are serious clinical choices, between blastocysts capable of developing further and those incapable of doing so, between blastocysts that will probably develop into healthy individuals and those that will not. Even the use of blastocysts in research should be governed by a serious therapeutic rationale and the well-grounded hope that it will lead to improvement in the welfare of individuals and the community. While the nature of these ethical choices is open to debate and a variety of applications, this is where serious theological reflection should be directed rather than at the use of blastocysts per se.

Additional criteria are that as much information as possible has been obtained from animal experiments before research using human embryos is contemplated, let alone commenced. In other words, any use of human embryos should be a last resort, and should not be used as long as viable alternatives remain. Any research endeavours should also be assessed within the broader framework of the legitimacy of the science itself. Is it skewing our attitudes? Are we, as societies, becoming too dependent on technological inroads into reproduction? Are we becoming obsessed with biological normality? Questions of this nature do not presuppose particular answers, but serve to make us cautious of technological imperialism.

It is also important that the implications of what we are doing are made explicit. If human embryos are destroyed, either clinically or in research, we appear to be assuming that these particular embryos are not made in the image of God and that God does not have a special love for them. If this assumption is incorrect, we should not be doing what we are doing. However, this is a far from novel situation, seeing that numerous human embryos are lost in all forms of reproduction, very often owing to chromosomal abnormalities. And in practice it is the fetuses that go on to become babies that we most revere, and not the extremely early embryos that (unknowingly) succumb. In IVF, most of the surplus embryos no longer required for reproductive purposes are eventually destroyed, suggesting that they are valued less highly than those that are now children. While the latter image God, what about those that end up surplus to requirements?

Some of these questions might seem to have a bizarre quality to them, in that they are employing terminology usually reserved for children and adults. This might suggest that the concept of "being in the image of God" does not apply to early embryos, and that to think in these terms is unhelpful. Peterson (2001) argues that there is no information about whether this image is present in the womb, although he appears to doubt that it is:

> If God's image means reflecting God in some way, learning to love as God loves or to seek truth as God is truth, then capability and choice become crucial to reflecting God's image ... The image of God would be available to all human beings but not present in all human beings. Every human being would be valuable and capable of bearing God's image, but not all would actually be doing so (p. 128).

Can we go back?

The issues that are emerging here appal some people, since from their perspective we should not be in this situation at all. We should return to a former time, when these intrusions into the reproductive sphere did not exist. A traditional perspective has been to err on the side of caution. Since early embryos *might* be full human persons, they should be protected and never exploited. Consequently, they should be neither studied nor treated in any manner that might jeopardise their best interests. Glen Stassen and David Gushee (2003) write:

> I would rather be wrong in attributing too much personhood to the fetus than in attributing too little. Surely the more pernicious tendency in human history has been to err on the side of

too much exclusion from covenant community rather than too much inclusion, with disastrous and cruel results.

Protection of the embryo is attained at the expense of all other interests, thereby eliminating the possibility of obtaining knowledge about our beginnings and any possibility of therapy that might arise from this knowledge. By its very nature, this position is also an ongoing one, since the possibility on which it is based will never be resolved.

This is a conservative stance, but is it an inherently Christian one? While it is certainly a possible position for Christians, it is not inherent in the general biblical principles referred to earlier. It also ensures that a Christian contribution to thinking in this area will be eliminated, since debate on the criteria to be employed in clinical and research procedures will proceed without Christian input unless Christians with this position are prepared to sit on committees with oversight of reproductive technologies and embryo research. It also has repercussions in clinical practice, where many procedures involve the destruction of early embryos, or rely on research using embryos – from post-fertilisation contraception and IVF and its many offshoots, to many attempts to understand and treat the causes of infertility. Consistency demands that Christians of this persuasion will have no involvement in such clinical practice.

Further afield, the entire scientific basis of embryology that is integral to the language and concepts of early human development stems from the study of human embryos over many years. In the eyes of some this type of study jeopardises the dignity of those particular embryos. These consequences are well illustrated by Hui (2002), with his rejection of the artificial reproductive technologies and artificial contraceptives. He argues that these technologies ask God to accept the child when he has not given that gift of life (p. 187).

While these comments in no way invalidate a conservative stance, they begin to show the choices that are being made, since as we have seen previously choices are inevitable. By assuming that every embryo is a human person and a full member of the human community, other members of that community (including possibly other embryos) will be deprived of access to therapies and procedures that might otherwise have been made available to them. Once again, it may be possible to justify this; my point is that this assumption about embryonic status has consequences for the human community.

Between certainties and uncertainties

All elements of this discussion have been on the borders of what might be described as *certainties* and *uncertainties*. These refer, respectively, to areas where we definitely know how we should act, and those where there is considerable doubt. In biblical terms, this is the distinction between areas where there is revealed teaching, and others where there is silence. The general principles outlined above fit in to the category of certainties, even if they do not take us as far as we would like. In these terms, viewpoints on the precise status of the embryo (regardless of which they are) fit into the category of uncertainties. Consequently, discussions of early human embryos will always be found at the borders of these two groups.

Unsatisfactory as this may sound, it is a familiar position for those of us writing on biomedical issues, on topics from the dead human body and human skeletal remains, to the retention and use of human organs and a range of human material, and on to the status of patients in a persistent vegetative state or with advanced dementia (Jones, 2000b). The challenge is to achieve a balanced perspective on all such bor-derline issues, especially as they relate to core certainties. For instance, there is much about embryonic life that we do not know, but we do know that embryos are not more important (theologically and ethically) than children or adults. We also know that embryos are more important than easily replace-able human tissues like skin and mucosa, because they have the potential to become like one of us. Wisdom lies in deter-mining this balance, wisdom that should inform everything from theological reflection through to a society's policies.

It is in these borderlands that comparisons are repeatedly being made between human embryos and other humans, between competing needs and aspirations. It is also important to remember that embryos should not dominate our thinking to the exclusion of everyone else. In the stem-cell area, most of the time and effort go into thinking about the harm that can be done to blastocysts, while ignoring the good that could be done to innumerable children and adults if some of the hopes about embryonic (let alone adult) stem cells came to reality. This is the balance between maleficence and benefi-cence (Peters, 2003a).

My contention is that, whatever specific decisions are made, the Christian ethos is to see people in their wholeness and treat them accordingly. This is where respect, dignity and preciousness in God's sight become operative for all humans, and not simply for any one group at the expense of all other groups. There will not be simple answers, and we have to be prepared to live alongside those who will adopt a different perspective from ours. In this context it is useful to bear in mind the words of the preacher in Ecclesiastes 11:5: "Just as you do not know how the breath comes to the bones in the mother's womb, so you do not know the work of God, who makes everything". We live in the midst of uncertainties, and on so many occasions our insights into the work of God are deficient. Balancing the welfare and aspirations of competing groups is far from easy, requiring discernment, wisdom and a willingness to go on learning in an ever-changing world. The perplexity of our beginnings will increase, rather than decrease, a truth amply illustrated by the debate surrounding stem cells. It is to this topic that we now turn.

Chapter 4

The Enigma and Challenge of Stem Cells

I n the previous chapter, I laid the groundwork for our thinking about human embryos. In this chapter I turn to the ways in which we should treat embryos. This, of course, flows on from how we think about embryos, since if we consider they are identical in status to all of us reading these words, we will wish to protect them under every possible circumstance. Hence, the possibility of using embryonic stem cells (ESCs) will prove untenable. On the other hand, if that is not our position, the world of ESCs will take on a different hue.

It is hardly surprising that the debate on stem cells has theological overtones. And yet the newness of the debate and the confusion that so often arises between stem cells and cloning means that the extent of the debate within Christian circles has been far less than one might have expected. It has also tended to be more diffuse and unhelpful than one would have hoped. Nevertheless, there is some history of attempts to address the cloning debate by theologians.

Theological reflections in the past

A very small number of theologians were discussing human cloning as long ago as the 1960s and 1970s, but these were the exceptions and even they had never contemplated stem cells. The newness of the topic is itself a cause for reflection. And so we should ask whether theologians were negligent in failing to discuss matters concerning stem cells many years ago, and, if they had done so, would the debate have been better informed now than it actually is?

With these questions in mind, it is interesting to look at the character of the cloning debate prior to the mid-1990s. Theologians such as Paul Ramsey, Joseph Fletcher and Richard McCormick were concerned with eugenic possibilities, human freedom, embodiment, our relationship with nature, and the meaning of parenthood (Ramsey, 1970; Fletcher, 1974; McCormick, 1981). While the stances of these writers differed markedly from one another, the debates did point to some important issues that are even more relevant today than they were then. However, perhaps inevitably, the background to the debates tended to be one of extremes. For some, science was about to lead humanity into a new world order and so should be welcomed; for others, any intrusion of technology into procreation was a threat to human standing before God and so should be rejected. However, the very broad context within which the debates were being framed at that time meant there was no way in which they could get beyond this crude polarisation.

Looking back from our perspective, 30 years on, it is clear that neither extreme position has eventuated. Science is now viewed in far more pessimistic and cautious terms than it was then, while some of the technology that Ramsey argued so firmly against has been with us for over 20 years. One is tempted to conclude, therefore, that those debates have had limited influence on current thinking, including current theological thinking, about the artificial reproductive technologies. However, the conservative tradition championed/upheld by Ramsey in opposition to cloning is a predominant force today in both secular and theological circles.

But what about stem cells? One cannot expect them to have been discussed by theologians before their therapeutic and research potential became a subject of interest to scientists in the late 1990s. However, the relationship between stem cells and embryos is another matter. Human embryos have been available for study in the laboratory since the early 1970s, when scientists first began their attempts at developing IVF procedures. However, with the exception of people like Ramsey and McCormick, it was many years before theologians paid much attention to this area. Their focus of interest was abortion and the fetus, not IVF and the early embryo. Consequently, when ESCs hit the headlines in 1998, the theological community was unprepared for the rapidly escalating debate that was to follow. This is because the abortion debate with its emphasis on the fetus is of little assistance in determining the manner in which early embryos such as five-to-seven-day-old blastocysts are to be treated. Alongside this, as we saw in the last chapter, the environment has shifted from the womb (*in vivo*) to the laboratory (*in vitro*).

The novelty of this move is startling. It has not previously entered the ambit of theological interest. Generally, it appears to have been accepted that an embryo is an embryo is an embryo. And so, if it is argued that personhood or full human value is acquired at fertilisation, differences in the location of embryos carry little, if any, theological weight. In a similar way, if the theological response to abortion is a negative one, it follows that the response to cloning and the use of ES cells will be equally negative. This is not to suggest that all theological responses are of this nature; as we shall see later in this chapter, they are not. My point is that any response that slides seamlessly from the older fetus to the early embryo, and from abortion to ESCs, is likely to be misleading. There is a biological gulf of immense dimensions between the two categories, a gulf that demands nuanced and precise theological understanding.

This is important, not only for the integrity of theological contributions, but also for the usefulness of such contributions in clinical contexts. Society at large, biomedical scientists, clinicians, and patients, need assistance in finding their way through the maelstrom of complex bioethical issues that characterise reproductive biology and reproductive medicine.

Embryonic stem cells

What are embryonic stem cells?

Human ESCs burst into the limelight in 1998, when they were first successfully derived. The attention they have subsequently received, on account of their potential to alleviate a range of debilitating illnesses and give rise to a new genre of medical therapies, has been bewildering (Towns & Jones, 2004a). These positive vistas have been counterbalanced by a welter of concerns, ranging from the ever-present ethical dilemmas precipitated by the moral status of the human embryo, to a confusing array of conflicting claims regarding the scientific superiority of adult stem cell (ASC) sources. What comes to the fore here is the balance between beneficence and maleficence, beneficence towards those with serious illnesses (who could possibly benefit from stem-cell therapies) and maleficence towards embryos (which would be destroyed in the act of extracting stem cells from them). Unfortunately, the place of beneficence is raised only occasionally in theological discussions of ESCs (an exception is Peters, 2003a and b).

It is now well recognised that stem cells are unspecialised cells, which have the ability to renew themselves indefinitely, and under appropriate conditions can give rise to a variety of mature cell types in the human body. They have multiple sources, ranging from embryos to umbilical cord blood, fetal tissues, and a variety of adult tissues. For the sake of simplicity, stem cells from all sources other than embryos are termed adult stem cells (as opposed to ESCs).

ESCs are usually derived from the ICM of early embryos at the blastocyst stage, which occurs at about five to seven days after fertilisation. As we saw in Chapter 3, at this point in time the blastocyst has differentiated into just two cell types, ICM cells and the surrounding trophectoderm cells (which will form the later placenta). The ICM cells are frequently considered to be totipotent, in that they have the capacity to give rise to a complete individual. However, this is only the case if the blastocyst, with its trophectoderm cells, is maintained in an intact state, and if it is eventually placed in a woman's uterus. Isolated ICM cells in the laboratory will not form a new individual. This means that ESCs are pluripotent, with an ability to create all the cell lines of the fetus but not the fetus itself.

What emerges from these considerations is that, within a laboratory environment, blastocysts are "potentially totipotent" rather than "actually totipotent" (Towns & Jones, 2004a). In this, they stand in stark contrast to their counterparts within a woman's body. Since the location of blastocysts is crucial scientifically, one has to ask whether this has ethical (and perhaps theological) connotations. Traditional ethical debate has taken no account of environmental considerations, its focus being entirely on blastocysts (embryos) as discrete autonomous entities, as though their potential to become future individuals can be realised regardless of environmental constraints.

A fundamental consideration is that, in order to obtain ESCs, the blastocyst has to be destroyed, since the ICM is disrupted. There is no way of obtaining ESCs and maintaining the blastocyst as a viable entity. Does this matter? Is the destruction of blastocysts at five to seven days after their formation unethical or even immoral? We are back at the moral status of the blastocyst. Or are we?

Did fertilisation take place? At present, the answer will be "yes", but in the future this might not always be the case. Theoretically, the blastocyst stage could be eliminated altogether. But that is not the situation at present. The question for now concerns the reasons why the blastocysts were created. This might have been specifically for research or therapeutic purposes, or they might be surplus to the requirements of couples in IVF programmes. In the former case, they were brought into existence in order to serve as research or therapeutic tools; their creation and destruction as a source of ESCs are intimately linked. In the latter case, they were created in an attempt to bring a new human being into existence; they are no longer required for this end and hence will be discarded; their creation and destruction as a source of ESCs are not linked.

In neither case is there an opportunity for these blastocysts to give rise to new individuals; their future life-giving role is non-existent. There is no intention that they should do so, while their laboratory environment ensures that they will not do so. Although extracting stem cells from blastocysts will destroy them, these particular blastocysts were slated for destruction anyway. The result is that decision-making will revolve around the respective merits of blastocysts that have been deprived of their life-giving ability, and of the benefits that might accrue to humanity from research and therapy using ESCs. There are ambiguities on both sides of this equation. The production of blastocysts that become available for use in ESC research, plus the research itself, have to be justified ethically, theologically and clinically. Neither is a value-free activity.

Embryonic and adult stem cells

In contrast, the process of obtaining stem cells from adult tissues is minimally invasive. The major adult tissue sources are bone marrow and blood, with fetal tissue also being included here. Hence, there is a major category difference between ESCs and ASCs, especially in ethical debate, where the adult variety is seen as being far less problematic morally than the embryonic variety. What this highlights is their source, for example, blastocysts versus skin cells or mucosa from adults. This is cut and dried, and yet the actual identification of stem cells depends to some extent on the environment. Indeed, there appears to be a dynamic relationship between all types of stem cell and their immediate microenvironment – the stem-cell niche (Watt & Hogan, 2000). The components of this microenvironment have an impact on stem cells, because they affect the precise directions in which they subsequently develop. In other words, both ASCs and ESCs demonstrate considerable plasticity.

One conclusion that could be drawn from this is that the plasticity of ASCs renders the use of ESCs unnecessary. However, there are a number of scientific reasons to suggest it would be unwise to draw this conclusion (Towns & Jones, 2004a). Even though there are a few confirmed reports of truly pluripotential human ASCs (National Institutes of Health, 2001; Committee on the Biological and Biomedical Applications of Stem Cell Research, 2002), what is required is far more understanding of the fundamental biological issues raised by this research. Scientifically, therefore, research with both adult and embryonic sources should continue, bearing in mind that ASCs are more problematic scientifically than their embryonic counterparts.

In view of this evaluation, considerable care should be employed in advocating, on allegedly scientific grounds, the advantages of adult over embryonic cells as the source of replacement tissues. In other words, it is short-sighted to attempt to circumvent discussion of the moral status of the blastocyst by concentrating on the scientific potential of ASCs alone.

While the use of ASCs may appear to be preferable to that of ESCs on ethical and theological grounds, this is only true (and then is debatable) if attention is concentrated exclusively on the embryo. This clear-cut preference is far less convincing as soon as the health needs of children and adults are taken into consideration. The therapeutic potential of stem cells, including ESCs, cannot be ignored by any who take the welfare of human beings seriously. This surely should be a theological imperative; to do good wherever this is feasible.

The balance between ASCs and ESCs is never static. It is in a state of flux. This depends in part on the precise state of scientific understanding, which is a crucial backdrop to social and theological deliberations. Another contributor to the flux is theological understanding itself. Fixated as much of this has been on fertilisation and "the point of conception", it now has to come to grips with embryonic events that are post-fertilisation, or even neo-embryonic events that lack any relationship to fertilisation (such as SCNT).

The traditional much-discussed time points are fertilisation and its major alternative, fourteen days post-fertilisation (with its primitive streak, end of twinning, and implantation into the wall of the uterus). However, each of these has major drawbacks when confronted by five-to-seven-day-old blastocysts. The challenge of this five-to-seven-day stage is its location at an intermediate time point between fertilisation and fourteen days, and both positions will have to incorporate it into their respective schemes. Theological thinking will also have to come to terms with this intermediate stage.

Current theological debate

While the diversity of theological debate is as great as ever, it has become more specific than the debate of the 1970s and 1980s. In order to provide an overview of the current state of this debate, I shall highlight three representative contributions (Jones, 2005). Since these are not confined to discussions of ESCs, we will have to retrace some of the ground covered in Chapter 3 on the more general issue of embryonic status.

Ethic of personhood based on relationality

The first position is that of Edwin Hui, Professor of Biomedical Ethics and Christianity and Chinese Culture at Regents College, Canada. His 2002 book *At the Beginning of Life: Dilemmas in Theological Ethics* contains an extended treatment of his position.

Hui's stress is on the organism's intrinsic goal-directedness, allowing him to conclude that the embryo is a complete autonomous human individual, and hence is a human person with the potential to develop. From this he concludes that the human soul is present at conception, and that the image of God expresses a unique relationship that is initiated, established and sustained by God from the embryonic stage and beyond. This, he claims, points to God's faithfulness in keeping a unilateral covenant of love and grace with every human individual. Consequently, all are persons irrespective of their inability to respond to God on account of developmental immaturity or disability, or their unwillingness on account of sinfulness.

One outworking of this framework is Hui's opposition to any technological inroads into the reproductive process, including the gamut of artificial reproductive technologies (ARTs), artificial contraceptives, embryo manipulation and surrogacy. In his view, use of ARTs forces God to accept the child when he has not given that gift of life, since technological reproduction replaces divinely initiated procreation. As a result, he vigorously opposes use of ESCs, since from his perspective this reflects a total disregard for the value of embryonic lives.

Hui describes his ethical position as one of personhood based on relationality, according to which changes and improvements are acceptable only where what has been created frustrates the Creator's intention for relationship. Any procedures that undermine our dependence on God and our interdependence on fellow human beings are unacceptable.

Hui's dual emphases on relationality and on a foundation based on God's purposes are welcome. But they lead to problems. The inadmissibility of any technological interference in reproduction leads to the conclusion that, in this domain, God only works through natural processes. However, similar reasoning in other branches of medicine would lead to the conclusion that life-saving operations and the use of antibiotics or antidepressants thwart the purposes of God. One has to ask why they appear to do this in the reproductive area but not in others; presumably because the origin of ontogenetic life is seen as being of a different character from the others. Second, it is difficult to understand why the birth of a longed-for child following artificial intervention and within a loving context is not a gift of God, while an unwanted child born naturally and not in a loving context is a gift of God. Third, he appears to limit the role of human intervention in reproduction, confining it to natural intercourse. Nowhere is scientific creativity allowed a supplementary role, even to enhance the natural process.

It is not clear how the theological principles enunciated by Hui are to be applied in pluralist societies. A set of ethical ideals is mapped out, based on a set of theological principles. Those who espouse these ideals and their social repercussions will encounter a major gap between them and most other positions within society. This is not a criticism of the ideals per se, but assistance is required to determine how Christians holding these ideals are to function in an alien environment. Hui does not provide a way forward (see Chapter 8).

The common nature of early embryos

The second position is that represented by two Roman Catholic bioethicists, Thomas A. Shannon and James J. Walter, in their 2003 book *The New Genetic Medicine*. Using various avenues the authors arrive at the conclusion that an individual is not present until about two to three weeks after the beginning of fertilisation, arguing that one cannot claim the moral relevance of individuality until after the process of restriction has occurred. Prior to that it is more appropriate to refer to the embryo's "common nature", when its genetic status is associated with what is common to all, not what is unique to a particular individual. This argument is partly dependent on what they see as the totipotency of the cells of the pre-implantation embryo, so that it is only when this capacity is lost through the process of restriction that an ontological individual emerges.

In view of these arguments, they are resolute in stating that the early embryo cannot claim absolute protection based on its claims to personhood; it is not an individual person from fertilisation. However, they are equally clear in asserting that the early embryo is valuable. This is based on the fact that it is living, has the human genetic code and possesses genetic uniqueness. Its value does not depend on the presence of characteristics like intelligence or a capacity for relationships.

Taken together, these arguments lead them to claim that

the pre-implantation embryo has what they describe as "pre-moral value". This pre-moral value must be judged in the light of other pre-moral and moral goods, such as the benefits that might accrue from research on these embryos in reproductive and other areas. In view of these underlying concepts, the authors are prepared to allow research on human embryos, including ESC research and therapy, and therapeutic cloning. Their conclusions are in striking contrast to Hui's, and demonstrate the divergence of opinion within Christian circles, even when the proponents of these viewpoints take biblical and theological contributions with the utmost seriousness.

While I have considerable sympathy with the position of Shannon and Walter, I have some reservations. Its emphasis on the totipotency of the pre-implantation embryo is nebulous, suggesting that a far greater range of cells is totipotent than appears to be the case. Additionally, the phenomenon of restriction probably occurs earlier than these authors suggest, and this might cast some doubt on the assurance with which they argue for the pre-individual status of the embryo throughout its first two to three weeks of development.

Embryonic dignity – conferred and claimed

The third position is that of Ted Peters, a Presbyterian theologian at the Center for Theology and the Natural Sciences in Berkeley, California. I shall refer to views expressed in his 2003 book *Playing God? Genetic Determinism and Human Freedom* (Peters, 2003a), and also to a review article in the journal *Theology and Science* (Peters, 2003b).

Peters is curious as to why so many theologians, when confronted by the value of the human embryo, are drawn to the past, since this confines the debate to what he considers is a confused account of genetic origin. He contends that this is not required by Christian theology, because it leaves out of the account God's eschatological call to become who we are destined to be. This is closely allied with gifts given us by God, namely, our creativity as human beings, the glimpse we have been given of God's promised future, and our ability to make decisions for the good. This is foundational for the major themes he outlines.

The first of these is *dignity*, which he sees as being initially conferred and subsequently claimed. Dignity is relational in character, in that it is the fruit of an ongoing loving relationship, expressed so clearly in the developing relationship between a mother and her newborn. This is where Peters' future orientation enters the picture, as he regards dignity as being derived more from destiny than from origin. The conferring of dignity on someone who does not yet experience or claim it is a gesture of hope. It is the future end product of God's saving activity rather than something imparted with the genetic code. This has ethical implications, in that we are to impute dignity to those who might not already experience it, enabling them to claim it for themselves.

A second characteristic of Peters' position is that, since the spotlight is no longer directed exclusively onto the early embryo, the principle of *beneficence* can be included in ethical calculations. This allows him to examine which other groups might benefit from a greater understanding of the embryo, emanating possibly from research on the embryo. Beneficence is important for Peters, because, with his future-directed gaze, he envisions a time when genetic medicine might promise a significant measure of potential for relieving crying and pain.

The promise contained within this vision can be brought about only by *creativity*. Peters argues that we cannot avoid being creative; what is important are the purposes towards which our creativity is directed. Since these include scientific advance in the reproductive sphere, we will inevitably come face to face with a range of choices in this sphere. Peters responds by stating that it is incumbent on us to construct ethical visions that take expanded choice of this nature into consideration. Such choices inevitably involve questions raised by genetic make-up; but, rather than seeing these exclusively in technological terms, he reminds us that any answer must incorporate the theological perspective that God loves each of us regardless of genetic make-up. Therefore, we are to do likewise.

One of the most provocative aspects of Peters' thesis is his discussion of the possibility that virtually any *somatic cell* within our bodies might be a potential human being. He is interested in asking how this might affect our view of the dignity of embryos, since it opens up the prospect that each cell in our bodies might one day acquire the status of a potential embryo. He wants to avoid ethical arbitrariness in giving a special status to some totipotent cells but not to others. This has direct relevance to stem cells, because if an embryo could be produced from a stem cell, it appears that all ethical concerns previously applying to the use of embryos in research would now apply to ESCs. While this is pushing beyond the bounds of current science, it serves to focus attention on whether the dignity currently ascribed to embryos might eventually have to be ascribed to any totipotent cell, and, if so, why.

Peters does not consider that individual human dignity is violated at the source of stem cells, leading him to conclude that the benefit of the doubt should be given to beneficence. Ethical encouragement should be given to proceed with this type of research.

We might ask whether this approach leads to the bestowal of differential value on human beings, in that some are valued more highly than others because some are provided with greater opportunities to flourish. Likewise, are embryos differentially valued, and are they as a group valued less highly than children and adults? The answers appear to be that there will be differential value, but it can also be argued that this is what happens in practice, no matter how much the absolute value of all humans from conception onwards is proclaimed. The Christian commitment should be to achieve as much equality as feasible for individuals, and to help provide conditions that will enable the human community as a whole to flourish.

Searching for a biblical contribution

Underlying every facet of this debate is a searching question for Christians, and this is what part biblical perspectives have to play in coming to a view of the meaning and value of the blastocyst and ESCs. Some general biblical themes were touched on in Chapter 3. But we now need to consider how these are used in reaching conclusions in applied areas. Consider the following possible categories: 1) the Bible alone provides a complete guide to ways in which blastocysts should be treated, making scientific input irrelevant; 2) the Bible is one of a number of sources of concepts and information, but emerges as the major determinant whenever there is conflict or confusion; 3) the Bible is irrelevant and hence can provide nothing of any interest to scientists or ethicists; 4) the Bible is one of a number of sources of concepts and information, and helps to inform decision-making, but might not be the major source.

It is difficult to see how category 1 can be upheld when the subject matter was unknown to the biblical writers. Blastocysts and ESCs are products of contemporary thinking.

Any direct reference to them in Scripture is impossible. On the other hand, many will argue that, if it can be shown that the human embryo is inviolable from conception, by definition blastocysts are also inviolable. Complete protection for blastocysts is mandatory; ESCs should be placed beyond the reach of scientists and clinicians. But does each of these assertions emerge from Scripture alone?

As outlined in Chapter 3, the view that the human embryo is inviolable from conception onwards relies heavily on the personal experiences of a limited number of people in the Bible (mainly David, the king, and Jeremiah, the prophet). As these servants of God looked back over their lives, they were able to recognise the goodness of God in protecting and supporting them through myriad circumstances, even those affecting their lives before birth. Such personal and specific references are interpreted by some as referring not only to the experiences of these particular people, but to all embryos. This move from the specific to the general is what I have referred to as the fallacy of interpreting retrospective statements in a prospective manner. This transformation removes them from category 1 to category 2. The biblical evidence may point towards the desirability of protecting embryos whenever possible, but the further move to inviolability is a leap beyond this. The personal history of God's servants is, principally, the personal history of God's servants. To make this into a general principle relating to the status of all embryos regardless of their relationship to a community of faith (Jones, 1987) requires reference to extra-biblical concepts.

In other words, most stances that are put forward as being entirely based on the Bible (category 1 in my terminology) are actually *category-2* positions. Take another example, that of Mary when she was first aware of Jesus before his birth (Luke 1:41–44). Some consider that, in view of this, Jesus' embryonic life confers a special significance on all other human beings, and also that all human embryos carry the rights and dignities that membership of the human species entails (Cameron, 1987). The latter is not implicit in the biblical evidence.

In a similar vein, the time spent by Jesus as an embryo has been used to argue for the Word becoming flesh down to the level of our genes. Since genes were unknown to the biblical writers, this is a theological statement reinterpreted in modern biological language. It has also been claimed that Jesus, in his role as mediator, has taken our human flesh into relationship with God in a decisively new way from conception onwards (Atkinson, 1987). This is used to demonstrate that human existence (personhood; the image of God) commences at conception, and therefore is inviolable, a statement which involves major extrapolation from the biblical testimony.

It is clear that those who claim to argue exclusively on biblical grounds (category 1) fail to do so, since other data and concepts are being introduced into these positions (placing them in category 2). The same applies to all arguments that are allegedly based on Scripture but use genetic uniqueness, a scientific notion, to bolster claims that human life (personhood) commences at conception. The belief that every human embryo ever conceived is to be protected is a possible, but not an inevitable, extension of biblical principles.

An excellent example of a category 2 writer is Hui (2002), whose position I examined above. As we saw there, he analyses in a serious manner a broad range of approaches to the embryo and allied reproductive technologies, and yet ultimately his approach appears to owe more to theological imperatives. His assurance regarding conception as God's creative act within a covenant of love and grace emanates from his theological commitment, which he then applies to every embryo ever conceived. Consonant with this, he allows a diminished role for science and scientific procedures. However, he recognises that biblical texts, viewed in isolation of other input, fail to provide a way forward when specific decision-making is required in contemporary debate.

None of the writers I am discussing falls into category 3, which is also a position I reject. Since category 3 reflects the stance of those whose starting point lies outside the Hebraic-Christian tradition, I shall not discuss it any further in this book.

The contributions of Shannon and Walter (2003) and Peters (2003a,b) fall into category 4. They start from well-formulated theological traditions, which they aim to utilise to inform current debates surrounding the blastocyst and ESCs. However, they accept that these traditions might require modification in the light of the latest scientific developments. In allowing this they are assuming that the traditions themselves incorporate scientific concepts, albeit ones dating from past centuries. While it is true that these writers have not set out to analyse the biblical writings, they take close note of what they regard as theological principles that emerge from biblical testimony and church tradition. They are prepared to examine possible repercussions of scientific explorations, such as the influence of the environment (including the laboratory environment) on the value to be ascribed to blastocysts, and incorporate these into their perspectives. Their horizons also include the welfare of the human community as a whole, and where blastocysts might fit in to this.

A danger inherent within category-4 positions is that scientific data might be misinterpreted and scientific concepts overextended, either of which will vitiate the scientific contribution and might distort the theological stance. This parallels the problems encountered in the category -1 and -2 positions, with their undue extension of biblical perspectives. A spirit of humility is essential, realising that there are vast unknowns and that the ground on which the debate is based is constantly shifting. But decisions have to be made, since the pressures for research and improved therapy will not disappear, and indeed should not disappear. It is in this spirit that I find myself most at home in category 4. Theologians (and Christians in general) do not have the luxury of arguing that the use of ESCs should not be contemplated until all the theological and ethical questions have been resolved to everyone's satisfaction. This is an unrealistic and unhelpful response.

Blastocysts and the human community

Category 4, with its assertion that the Bible is one of a number of sources of concepts and information in determining the value of the blastocyst and ESCs, rather than the source, will alarm many Christians. However, it is hardly radical. It is of a kind with our approach to many other facets of human existence, whether human nutrition, immunology, public health, or community issues. While Christian perspectives are relevant in each case, we would find it strange if asked to outline which specific biblical principles (let alone texts) constituted the bedrock of these approaches. And yet, aberrations in any of these areas can have devastating consequences for the welfare of individuals and whole communities. In other words, human existence is readily devalued when essential nutritional and immunological principles are ignored, or when clean water supplies are unavailable, overcrowding is rampant, infectious diseases are uncontrolled, and social cohesion breaks down. Christian contributions come into their own when Christians, committed to the dignity and worth of every human being, set out to provide the basic necessities for a healthy life in these areas, melding practical assistance and essential Christian values.

This provides a working model for approaching the human blastocyst and the derivation of ESCs. The dignity and worth of all in the human community are to be brought into focus, even though conflict will sometimes arise between what may appear to be competing interests. Peters' (2003b) emphasis on claiming the dignity initially conferred by God is important here, since it applies as much to disadvantaged children and adults as it does to blastocysts. From this it follows that, if it proves impossible to act in a beneficent manner towards all, a balance has to be found between maleficence and beneficence. In Christian language, one is striving for neighbour love – our neighbour being all in need, anyone whom we are in a position to assist. Examples include the patient with a debilitating disease, the person who has been abused, and the child with limited opportunities. Within this range of responsibilities, where do blastocysts feature? Are they in need in the way in which these others are in need, or is their protection the only relevant need?

Blastocysts are part of the human community, and yet they give the impression of occupying a different stratum from most others within this community. This is the root of our theological and ethical problems. They are ambiguous entities, regardless of what perspective one adopts towards them. The point I am making is that they never exist in isolation from others, even in the laboratory. Their continued existence and their further development depend upon others within this community and on a whole host of relationships. As we saw in Chapter 3, there are two main responses to this observation. Their weakness and vulnerability demand their complete protection. Since they are so totally dependent on others, they should be protected from ever being utilised in research or therapy. An alternative is to assess their worth alongside that of others within the human community. This leads to recognising their worth as a comparative one. But this has numerous ramifications in both ethical and theological terms, since they can no longer be provided with absolute protection (even theoretically). They will be assessed along with other demands made on the human community, demands that require all sorts of human decision-making, responsibility and control. Does this have ramifications for the moral status of embryos? Is it threatened or is it unaffected?

My argument is that environmental factors have to be taken into account in determining the fate of blastocysts and the availability of ESCs. A distinction has to be made between "blastocysts within an environment congenial to further development" and "blastocysts within an environment hostile to further development". Blastocysts are found naturally, as well as artificially, in a range of environments, some of which enhance their ontogenetic development, whereas others hinder it. In other words, some blastocysts possess the inherent, as well as environmental, potential to become flourishing individuals; others lack this potential on one or other score.

It is possible to reject such a distinction and contend that isolated blastocysts have an inherent value in and of themselves. Their environment is irrelevant, even if they are unable to develop further. Their inherent potential demands that they be placed in a suitable environment; to deprive them of the latter is akin to depriving a child of oxygen. While this cannot be completely denied, there is a difference, namely, that a suitable environment for a blastocyst's development is an inherent part of what it is. It is not an add-on. The trophectoderm is part of the blastocyst and not an external appendage. Hence, in the absence of trophectodermal cells, and of a uterus in which to implant, the remaining cells of the blastocyst lack the potential to develop into a human individual. And so, we have to ask what for many Christians is an unpalatable question. Is commitment to all blastocysts, irrespective of their environment, mandatory for Christians?

One answer to this question is an unequivocal "yes". Blastocysts have to be treated as persons, even though there are no scientific means of providing meaningful information that leads to this conclusion. This position bypasses the precise environmental conundrum I have just raised, because the underlying contention is that there is a vital relationship between God and embryos, conferring on embryos their unique status. But is this adequate when confronted by blastocysts that lack the potential for growing into the fullness of humanity, thereby suggesting that God has a vital relationship with innumerable blastocysts that will never be able to develop beyond a few days?

If God does have such a relationship with every blastocyst, the resulting Christian position is that it is incumbent on humans to provide the most congenial environment for the further development of every single blastocyst. Consequently, all blastocysts should be transferred to a woman's uterus, including possibly non-viable blastocysts and those with deleterious genes, no surplus embryos should be produced in IVF programmes, blastocysts should never be studied *in vitro* in the laboratory, and any form of ESC work is invalidated. The only legitimate Christian option is one characterised by opposition to embryo research and ESC-based therapies, as epitomised by Hui (2002).

However, once the blastocysts' environment is taken into consideration, the theological imperative changes. God is not viewed as being committed to every blastocyst; neither is he seen as having a special relationship with every blastocyst. The emphasis shifts to regarding God's call as a way of viewing people, not a means of understanding human development (McCarthy, 1997). There is explicit acceptance that there is no way of knowing whether every embryo is called (MacKay, 1984). We can agree that all people who are called were once embryos, and it would seem were called as embryos, but those who never made it beyond embryos remain an enigma. From this, we should perhaps be cautious in interfering with developing human embryos, but unless we adhere to the precautionary principle whereby the benefit of doubt is always to be given to the embryo (Stassen & Gushee, 2003), research on some embryos will not be categorically ruled out. Nevertheless, the dignity and worth of embryos will act as a major constraining force in what is done to and with them, on account of God's commitment to human tissue and all forms of human life (Jones, 1994). This will lead to very demanding standards for any scientific work that is envisaged, with decision-making taking account of the good of the human community as a whole. In particular, if blastocysts are brought into existence to serve as the source of tissues and cell lines, the *intentions* and *goals* of this procedure will have to be even more closely scrutinised.

Theology, public policy and embryonic stem cells

The relevance of the positions outlined above can be ascertained by assessing where they stand in relation to public policy on ES cells. As one scans the regulations worldwide, four dominant positions emerge (Towns & Jones, 2004b). These vary from position A, the prohibition of all embryo research, to position D, the creation of human embryos specifically for research – encompassing both fertilisation and SCNT. In addition, there are two intermediate positions. Of these, position B confines the use of ESCs to those currently in existence, in that they were extracted before some specified date, thereby prohibiting the extraction of ESCs and the utilisation of ESCs derived in the future. Position C allows for the use and ongoing isolation of ES cells from surplus IVF embryos.

Do these positions have any theological correlates? Position A, which is generally adopted by those in categories 1 and 2, is compatible with the stance that human life commences at fertilisation, allowing nothing to be done to the embryo that is not in its best interests. Such a stance would be expected to disapprove of IVF, on the grounds that its development and further refinement have necessitated research on embryos. Further, IVF programmes that incorporate the creation of surplus embryos would also be unacceptable, since these programmes inevitably result in the production of numerous embryos that will be discarded. By the same token, this position fails to contribute to any research or subsequent therapy dependent on the use of ESCs. Hence, it suffers from the neglect of any interests beyond those of the very early embryo. This fails to do justice to the obligations of servanthood, living in community, loving one's neighbour as oneself, and seeking to bring healing and wholeness to those in need.

In order to allow some research using ESCs, position B has been formulated, by allowing research only on stem cell lines already in existence. In other words, the embryos from which these lines were extracted have already been destroyed; that is a *fait accompli*. However, in an attempt to protect embryos in the future, this position forbids the destruction of any further embryos. In one stroke it gives the impression of placating both sides of an exceedingly contentious argument. Research can continue in a limited way, and some good might emerge from this research. It is not deaf to the plight of people with severe degenerating conditions that could, possibly, benefit from scientific advances. What is more, those advocating protection of human embryos can feel that their case has been supported, by preventing the destruction of any more embryos for research (and possibly therapeutic) purposes.

How should this compromise position be viewed theologically? Christians who view human life as commencing at fertilisation have reacted in two contrasting ways. One school of thought has berated the position on the grounds that it gives away too much. In their eyes it appears to accept embryo destruction, even though it is past destruction. For this school of thought position A is the only theologically acceptable position (this tends to be the position of those aiming to be category 1 people). In contrast, a second school of thought has welcomed the compromise as a way of taking science seriously while also protecting the interests of embryos (perhaps more akin to category 2 thinking).

The striking feature of position B is that, while it is based on the moral unacceptability of embryo destruction, it allows the use of existing cell lines. Since these have been obtained through the destruction of embryos, the policy implicitly accepts the legitimacy of embryo destruction, albeit in the past. If this were not the case, no research of any description utilising human embryos or ESC lines would be tolerated. Position A, with its prohibition of any such research, would be the stance of choice. On the other hand, an unwillingness to move to position C, permitting the extraction and utilisation of ESCs, demonstrates that the destruction of human embryos is deplored. Position B represents an uneasy compromise, made possible only by accepting the use of "ethically tainted/unethically derived" material (Towns & Jones, 2004b). It is also inconsistent, because the societies advocating this position allow the production of surplus embryos in IVF programmes; embryos are not being protected. Restrictive ES cell guidelines serve only to prevent research on embryos that will be destroyed anyway; and it will probably hamper scientific research (Towns & Jones, 2004a,b). Under these circumstances, there appear to be no reasons for not using surplus embryos for research purposes, including extracting ESCs (position C).

While the intentions of those advocating position B are admirable, the compromise is unsuccessful, in that it fails to satisfy either side. It sits very uneasily alongside ESC research and whatever therapies might eventually emanate from it. In view of this, position C emerges as having much to commend it, even though it lacks the absolute façade of position A. These two positions bring out the dimensions of the debate, highlighting as they do the contrast between treating the blastocyst as an isolated entity (A) or as an entity in community (C).

Position C provides a protective view of the human embryo, within the framework of a more consistent ethical stance. This is because ESC research is limited to surplus embryos from IVF programmes, with a procedural separation between the initial decision to discard embryos and the subsequent decision to donate them for research. This allows both the utilisation and the extraction of new ESCs, and eliminates arbitrary time limits on extraction. It also encompasses explicit acceptance of the therapeutic possibilities of ESC research.

While position D, with its allowance of the creation of blastocysts specifically for research and therapeutic purposes, is another possibility, the theological and ethical issues it raises are complex and are beyond the scope of the present chapter.

Contrasting perspectives

This is deeply ambivalent territory, and the pressure to prevent human embryos being demeaned (and ESCs utilised) is understandable. However, there has to be compelling theological evidence for advocating this negative stance. Within a Christian framework the following appear to play a crucial role in arriving at this stance:

1. There is explicit biblical evidence against the destruction of human embryos.
2. The thrust of the theological evidence is against the destruction of human life, including any pre-natal human life
3. The realm of the human embryo and human procreation should be left entirely as God's domain, and therefore should be off-limits to human-initiated intrusions.
4. Protection of human embryos outweighs efforts to improve the health of other humans.
5. The destruction of human embryos will have negative consequences for attitudes towards human life in general, and will lead to a culture of death.
6. Scientific inroads into the human person, by manipulating early developmental stages, will have long-term negative consequences for humanity.

Of these six points, 1 is an interpretation of the biblical evidence, while 2, 3 and 4 are theological statements. Numbers 5 and 6 are predictions of what might occur in the wake of continuing scientific work. When viewed as a package, the overall effect of these assertions is negative, with little indication that anything positive could emerge from ESC investigations. The distinct impression is that the world would be a better place without any of these developments.

I remain to be convinced that there is biblical teaching or adequate theological rationale for opposing ESC investigations under every conceivable circumstance. While reasons 5 and 6 should not be dismissed out of hand, the manner in which they are frequently expressed is far more assured than can be justified. Nevertheless, the deeply ambivalent nature of the territory demands caution at every level.

Adopting a positive stance, and proceeding with ESC work also requires theological and scientific justification:

1. There is no specific biblical teaching against it.
2. The thrust of the theological evidence is that pre-natal human life is of considerable value, and this should be assessed alongside the very considerable value of all human life.
3. The realm of the human embryo and human procreation comes within the ambit of human creativity, as humans demonstrate elements of God's own creativity.
4. Theological vistas need to be grounded in the future as well as the past, in hope as well as fear, in God's purposes as well as human frailty.
5. The outcome of ES cell research could have major benefits for the human community overall.
6. The degree to which manipulating the early stages of human development will be beneficial or counter-productive will depend on the goals to which it is directed: to benefit human welfare or serve unrealistic grandiose ends.

These reasons parallel the first set, and highlight the contrasting vistas. The biblical and theological basis is tipped towards the legitimacy of humans exercising control over the early stages of human existence, reflecting their creation in God's own image. Consequently, human responsibility comes far more to the fore, even while acknowledging that this can be abused and misdirected in a sinful world. Hence, a balance has to be sought between the possible range of negative and positive repercussions, enormous care being required to ensure that legitimate exploitation of the pluripotential nature of ESCs is not obtained at the expense of unethical exploitation of human blastocysts.

Both sets of responses represent valid Christian stances, each with its own emphases and each with somewhat different perspectives on the relationship between God's initiative and human initiative. They highlight the varying extents to which scientific contributions are allowed to influence applied theological understandings, the different roles envisaged for the blastocyst as a contributing member of the human community, and the extent to which the blastocyst should be treated as an individual human subject or as belonging to a more special subcategory of human tissue. These differences will determine the nature of our commitment to blastocysts compared to other humans within the human community, and whether we are prepared to allow the creation of artificially produced blastocysts to serve as the source of therapeutically directed tissues.

Chapter 5

The Human Person: Is Neuroscience a Danger to Our Well-being?

For most people, the brain is a fascinating yet perplexing organ. It is an organ unlike any other in the body, since it is "me" in a way in which my liver, kidneys or pancreas is not me. Our brains appear to make us the sort of people we are, and this is why there is general interest in the brains of people like Einstein and Lenin. The feeling is that their brains will provide clues as to what made them the outstanding people they were. The other side of the coin is what happens to us as people when something goes wrong with our brains. The harsh reality is that we might be dramatically changed, since certain forms of damage can have major repercussions for our personalities. The person whom we knew and instantly recognised as Richard or Grace may no longer be that same person; remnants of the person undoubtedly may remain, but the interactions we cherished and lived for might have vanished completely.

Well-known and tragic examples of what can go wrong abound in the neurological literature. Think of Phineas Gage, who was a construction foreman working on a new railway line in 1848. Tragically, an accidental explosion propelled a metre long iron rod through his skull and the frontal lobes of his brain. Unbelievably, Gage was not killed, and recovered from his injury. However, he was now a new person. Before the accident he had been soft-spoken, purposeful, capable and efficient; after the accident he became obstinate, rude, violent, and profane. Those who knew him concluded that he was "no longer Gage". For the remaining twelve years of his life, Gage was a living monument to the fact that personality can be dramatically transformed by destroying part of the brain, in his case the frontal lobes.

And then there is Zasetsky, a young soldier who was hit in the head by a bullet during the Russian offensive against the Germans in the Battle of Smolensk in 1943. His brain injury affected almost all facets of his existence. Initially he was unable to perceive anything, as his world had collapsed into fragments and he was unaware of the existence of the right side of his body. He had forgotten how to carry out day-to-day tasks such as how to shake hands, or how to thread a needle. He had also forgotten the names of common objects, got repeatedly lost, and had become illiterate. In many respects Zasetsky had been killed on that day, because his existence thereafter became a kind of half-sleep, or living nightmare. From that day onwards, by his own admission, he had become a different person. He described his state in these words: "I'm not a man but a shadow, some creature that's fit for nothing" (Luria, 1975).

Closer to the present day there is the case of a schoolteacher who began collecting sex magazines and visiting pornographic websites (Swerdlow & Burns, 2003). At some stage in a tragic sequence of events that led to his arrest, he was found to have a brain tumour pressing on his right frontal lobe. Removal of this tumour led to a reversal of his behaviour, suggesting the strong possibility of a direct relationship between this pathology and his antisocial behaviour. However, even more convincing evidence emerged with the subsequent regrowth of the tumour, and a reversion to this antisocial behaviour. Yet another operation saw his pornographic urges subside for a second time.

What does one make of these and many other similar illustrations? Quite simply, when things go wrong with our brains, as in these pathological situations, normal brain function can be seriously distorted. This was the situation in each of these examples. As obvious as this is, it should remind us that we do not work from the abnormal to the normal. Some behaviours are, indeed, neurologically determined, but we should not conclude from this that all behaviours are determined in just the same way (Jeeves, 2003).

Nevertheless, there is a close relationship between our brain and our behaviour. But why does this surprise us? Our thinking, emotions, responses and memories must have some physical basis, and this is in the brain. The only alternative to this is to postulate that they emanate from outside our bodies, or from some non-physical source. I can find no evidence for either of the latter, and so we have to take the brain and its various regions very seriously for an understanding of what we are as people.

The brain and personhood

In one sense, the brain is no different from any other organ we might care to mention, in that it can be described, dissected and understood in anatomical and physiological terms just like any of the other organs. But it also eludes us, simply because our view and knowledge of the world and ourselves are *products* of our brains. It is because of the organisation of our brains that we are able to love and pray, to create and enjoy beautiful things, and even to believe and worship. The development of the cerebral hemispheres means we can think in abstract terms, plan ahead and ponder the significance of the past; we have values and goals, and are aware of our responsibility for ourselves and other people; we know we are transient, and we can communicate not only with each other but also with God.

But have I overemphasised a mere physical structure? Surely, some will argue, we are more than our brains, in the same way that we are more than our genes? There is something grander about human beings than a mere physical object that, after death, we can preserve and keep in a bottle or box. True, the brain may be important, but doesn't it have to be seen in the context of something immaterial and more substantial? For some commentators, human personhood is viewed as a social and moral construct, because a person has to be far more than the underlying biological substratum. This is one way of saying that the functioning of our brains must be only a part of what we are as whole persons. There must be something additional, something that makes us the real people we are; something that transforms us from mere animals into spiritual beings capable of communicating with God. Wonderful as the brain is, it is not sufficiently wonderful to explain what our real essence is.

I have sympathy with this sentiment, because it is all too easy to reduce everything we are to a mere physical object. It is reductionism of this type that claims "We are *nothing but* our brains" or "*nothing but* our bodies". Forget all that is wonderful about human life; remember, we are *only* physical units, we are *only* machines. In the face of such reductionistic claims, one cannot blame people for objecting, and even, on occasion, for going to the opposite extreme and claiming that our brains are unimportant appendages. We are really non-physical beings, who happen to have brains (not to mention kidneys, stomachs and hearts).

Both extremes are unhelpful, because both overlook the obvious. We are conscious beings who have goals, desires and responsibilities. Our brains are fundamental to all we are, but it is *we* who are significant; it is *we* who are interested in understanding ourselves (and our brains); it is *we* who strive to be designers of the future. Damage to our brains might have devastating consequences for all we are and hope to be, pointing to the indispensable role played by them in making us what we are. But it is *we* who have meaning, not our brains. Consequently, personhood, that which makes us the people we are with all the potential we have, is more than brain activity per se. Nevertheless, there is an indissoluble link between the two.

One way of looking at this link is to return to the ongoing debate on ethical issues surrounding human embryos (see Chapter 3), since this has inadvertently brought into focus varying perspectives on the relationship between personhood and the nervous system (see Jones, 1998). This is because there is no hint of a nervous system in any early embryo (and this is unquestionably true up to 21 days or so of development).

According to one position, to be a human being is to be a person, even at the very earliest stages of human existence (Iglesias, 1987). Hence, personal abilities, including self-awareness, responsibility and creativity, are all potentially present from the earliest stages of development. Since there is no indication of a nervous system for the first three weeks of development, this position inevitably leads to the conclusion that a nervous system has no relevance for an understanding of personhood. If it is accepted that developing entities are persons, even in the absence of rudimentary nervous systems, the later emergence of complex nervous systems adds nothing of ethical or theological interest.

It's a short step from this to the position that, if we are persons throughout our history, we have special responsibility for the weakest and most needy members of the human community (Meilaender, 1996). These include early embryos, which are to be cared for as we seek to discover in their "faces" the face of Christ. Once again, there is no reference to any neurobiological criteria, which by implication are of no consequence. Personhood has become isolated from any neural considerations, as though the brain is an unimportant peripheral to human existence. The problem here is that any position of this ilk has no place for physical criteria when attempting to distinguish between different forms of treatment in ambiguous ethical situations.

A related perspective is that a person is neither a genetic nor a biological category, again rendering neuroscience irrelevant. The significance of people is said to emerge by interacting with them and by committing ourselves to them and their welfare (O'Donovan, 1984). It is on this basis that we come to realise that all human beings, including embryos, fetuses and the severely handicapped, are irreplaceable. Central to this stance is a commitment to persons, a notion that I regard as extremely valuable. Unfortunately, it's vague when isolated from appropriate neurobiological data.

Attempts such as these that ignore neurobiological considerations contain within them helpful general pointers for ethical decision-making. However, their reluctance to accept that scientific criteria help to direct our moral gaze seriously limits their applicability in real-life situations. Such criteria are necessary if we are to appreciate when a nervous system does or does not exist with sufficient material complexity to embody those capacities judged morally pertinent.

Clearly, a dead body with a non-functioning brain is no longer a person. We might wish to bestow some of the marks of personhood on that body on account of our memories of the person who once lived, but these are our memories and the status is imputed. In this instance, there is no escape from scientific criteria, whether cardiovascular or neuroscientific ones. In similar vein, neuroscientific considerations seem to be valuable when assessing the effects of severe brain damage on someone's personality. But why do this if an understanding of brain function lacks any relevance for what we are as people? In light of the illustrations at the beginning of this chapter, this position strikes me as untenable. More controversially, some would argue that the same applies at the very earliest stages of human life, when the presence of a rudimentary brain is a determinant of when the embryo or fetus is to be treated as a morally relevant being.

In other words, a scientific study of the nervous system by itself will not tell us all we want to know about people and their functioning. And yet, when confronted by a barely functioning brain, on account of immaturity at the beginning of life or degeneration at the end of life, neural activity cannot be ignored. The lack of any functioning of the central nervous system, no matter what state one's body is in, must have implications for our assessment of the meaningfulness of that human life. It seems to me that these extreme situations provide a useful starting point for demonstrating the intimate relationship between brains and persons.

Are brains machines?

But once we accept that the brain is an essential element in our thinking about persons, we introduce what for some people is the forbidding dictum that if an individual's brain is changed, that individual will be changed. If this is so, does the individual amount to no more than his or her brain? If this is even remotely the case, what becomes of humans as free agents? The impression is readily gained that they have lost all that is special about them; their very essence has disappeared, and the foundation on which their relationship with

God is based has been eroded. These are understandable concerns, but they are based on a *machine-type model* that suggests fixity and rigidity.

This introduces an idea similar to the one we encountered when looking at the notion of designer babies, with its basis in images of the factory-line production of babies (see Chapter 2). The pervasive model is again that of a machine, but on this occasion an internal machine rather than an external one – one that is directing us rather than producing us. The only solution, according to some, is to eliminate this machine-like unit (that is, the brain) from our understanding of personhood. I have already stated that this would be a mistake, since it results from a grave misunderstanding of the nature of brain function. Let's look at this in a little more detail.

The brain is the antithesis of a machine, simply because it is highly responsive to numerous environmental stimuli at all stages of life. The two-way interactions between the brain and the worlds internal and external to the individual point to the richness of its multidimensional context. In no sense can the brain be isolated from an individual, in the way in which the heart can be; neither could it be replaced by another brain without destroying the integrity of the individual as the person he or she is known to be. Let's undertake a thought experiment. Imagine four friends. Paul has had a kidney transplant, Mark has had a heart transplant, Ruth has an artificial hip, and Crystal has a "brain transplant". How might we respond to these four individuals, all of whom we know quite well? We have no problem recognising and relating to Paul, Mark and Ruth. In fact, they are probably far healthier than before their respective operations. We could say that they are back to "their old selves", since their illnesses had reduced them to invalids. Now they are "normal" again. But what about Crystal? She is no longer the person she once was. Her body is the same; we recognise her facial features, but her personality has changed. If we had known Sandy, whose brain Crystal now has, we might say she is more like Sandy than Crystal. We still have Crystal with us, but we have also lost her. All the experiences that made Crystal the person she was have gone, the memories have gone, the values and interests have changed; Crystal is a "changed person".

This is absurd science fiction, but I hope it helps to make the point that it is erroneous to regard ourselves as *consisting of* a brain, various other organs, and an immaterial "something" that constitutes the real me, whether this be mind or soul. On the contrary, our brains *represent* us. They make us what we are, but only in the sense that we also make *them* what *they* are. Far from being a machine-based model, this is a personal model. As we have seen before when dealing with genetics, a *personal model* is far more in line with a Christian perspective.

Brain plasticity and the person

In developing a *personal model* of the brain we need to look more closely at the brain itself, and in particular at one of its features, its plasticity (this is the term used by neuroscientists to denote flexibility and pliability). Once we do this, we realise that what we are as persons is not laid down once and for all in the genome. While it is true that the basic ground plan for an individual's brain is specified in the genome, the detailed patterns of synaptic connections that link its innumerable nerve cells (neurons) are fashioned by a host of influences throughout life (Jones, 2004a).

The developmental period is characterised by an initial overproduction of nerve cells, when there is massive competition between them, so that only about half survive into adulthood. The significant influence here is the external environment, since it is this that determines which synaptic connections between nerve cells persist and, therefore, which nerve cells will survive and flourish. For example, the eyes of the newborn must receive visual stimulation from the environment during the early months in order to fine-tune the structure of the visual part of the cerebral cortex (Eisenberg, 1999). In addition, this stimulation must occur at specified times (the so-called critical periods of brain development), revealing yet again the extensive influence that external inputs have on the end product that is the adult brain, and hence the adult individual.

Any disruption to these extrinsic factors will impact negatively on nerve-cell development and may grossly disturb the organisation of the brain, leading possibly to long-term neurological deficits (Levitt *et al.*, 1998). Change the environment, delay when sensory impulses arrive during development, and the resulting brain is different from what it would have been under other conditions. This is why malnutrition, alcohol and hormonal influences during pregnancy can have such devastating consequences for a child's subsequent intelligence and behaviour. In other words, influences of many types have profound repercussions on the physical organisation of the brain, and affect what we become as individuals and as persons.

It is the specific fine-tuning of the synaptic connections in any given brain that contributes substantially to that individual's uniqueness and personhood, fine tuning that occurs initially over the crucial period from six months' gestation to two years post-natal. After this, it continues throughout life as synapses are lost and replaced in all parts of the brain. The variation possible is well nigh infinite, and the connections are modified in response to all the experiences that constitute our lives as individuals. Our memories, our learned responses and our attitudes modify synaptic connections and the inter-actions of numerous nerve cells. At any one time, the form of the brain's neural organisation with its synapses and neural network depends on the environment just as much as on genetic factors. In other words, environmental influences are integral to the form of our brains and, therefore, to important features of what we are as persons.

Consequently, two individuals with identical genetic backgrounds will differ, depending on the spiritual and intel-lectual culture in which they are brought up, the religious influences on them, and innumerable facets of family life and the expectations of family, friends and society (Jones, 2001). This is made possible by the plasticity of their brains, and the continuously changing forms of their brains in response to the pressures of their environments. And what is true of iden-tical twins is true of every one of us. Very simply, without characteristics like these we would not be human persons. If we lacked them, we would be unable to respond to God.

Extensive plasticity like this makes possible the enor-mous range of human beings' intellectual abilities and spiri-tual gifts. It also opens up exciting therapeutic vistas, since it may prove possible to exploit the newly discovered regenera-tive possibilities. The extent of this regeneration is far more extensive than anything thought possible a few years ago, leading to optimism regarding ways of treating what up to now have been debilitating neurodegenerative diseases (such as Parkinson's disease and even Alzheimer's disease) and trauma (especially damage to the spinal cord). However, care is needed even here, since some erroneously conclude that we will be able to live lives that are both disease-free and of indef-inite length. Such expectations are absurd. While it is entirely appropriate to seek better treatment for debilitating and tragic diseases, the nature of human existence will not be revolutionised. The essence of regeneration is to rectify what has gone wrong, rather than bring about some new (and superior) way of functioning. Whatever is accomplished in the foreseeable future is likely to be limited, even though one hopes that these limited prospects will prove beneficial for numerous patients.

Intrusions into the brain

The plasticity of the brain makes it amenable to being modified for therapeutic and possibly other reasons. For instance, it is possible to transplant brain tissue from (aborted) human fetuses into patients with Parkinson's disease. Since the aim is to overcome the movement deficits experienced by these patients, the transplanted brain tissue is tissue that is responsible for motor control. Results have been of limited success in clinical terms, and the approach remains an interesting if experimental one (see Jones & Galvin, 2004, for a review).

But does transplanting brain tissue like this have implications for patients' views of themselves? Does it in any significant way alter what they are as people? When tissue is grafted into the motor regions (striatum) of the brain, it seems that such fears are unjustified, although this might not be the case if there were to be direct involvement of brain regions implicated in the expression of personality and emotional traits, such as the frontal and temporal lobes.

It appears that a nerve cell's significance stems from its functional capabilities and from the connections and circuits of which it is an integral part. If this is the case, the important factors are the nerve cells, growth factors and transmitters being transplanted, and the brain regions involved (Jones & Sagee, 2001). The origin of the nerve cells might be far less significant, whether from the same person, another person, or (very dramatically and surprisingly) even from different species. This is because what seems to be of paramount importance is the environment and context within which nerve cells develop and function. These together appear to determine an individual's ultimate personality. A statement like this is not claiming that one can do anything one likes to someone's brain; that is palpably not true. Enormous care is required when interfering with a person's brain. Nevertheless, these possibilities underlie the immense plasticity of our brains.

From current evidence it is clear that the presence of someone else's nerve cells inside our brains does not make us different people. The pivotal consideration is whether the procedure enhances or diminishes the individual as a person, not whether the graft comes from human fetuses, or even from the brains of young rats or pigs (but this raises additional considerations). It is the person as a self-reflective and self-knowing being who is important, and not what goes to make that person's brain function. If there is no essential difference between the person before and after a neural transplantation operation, the graft does not pose a threat to the integrity of what that person is and stands for.

This is an important principle that would also apply to the introduction of other cells or even computerised devices into the brain. If we know what that individual was like as a person prior to this operation, we have a baseline for comparing its effects on the individual in question. In what ways has the implant affected the person? If there is general agreement that Grace has "returned to her old self", or that deficiencies have been rectified, the improvement in health and in cognitive function is to be welcomed. Conversely, if much of what John once stood for and his dominant interests have been replaced by a meaningless existence, something has gone seriously wrong, even if his memory or eyesight have been lifted to new levels. What are some of these other implants that are on the horizon?

Neural transplantation is a relatively unsophisticated means of improving brain function. Far more precise methods are being actively investigated, including the use of stem cells, neural progenitor cells and gene therapy, all of which will probably contribute to the growing armamentarium of neural repair initiatives. The therapeutic potential of these approaches is generally discussed in the context of finding ways of tackling the major (and frequently devastating) neurodegenerative conditions that afflict growing numbers of people. It is unfortunate that discussion so often centres on finding cures for conditions like Parkinson's disease and Alzheimer's disease. As wonderful as it would be to achieve such cures, hype like this tends to be unhelpfully idealistic. Even Parkinson's disease, which is far more amenable to a cure than Alzheimer's disease, will be conquered gradually and probably in fitful and very tentative steps. And it might never be completely cured once it has taken hold and large numbers of nerve cells have died.

What is important from our perspective in this book is that even the merest hint that therapies might emerge is made possible by a fundamental belief (or postulation, if you like). This is that there is now substantial evidence that what we are as persons is not set indelibly at some early stage in our lives. Our brains are able to change momentously throughout life, signifying that what we are as persons is also amenable to considerable change. Our brains change and therefore we change. And, by the same token, we change and therefore our brains change. There is an intimate connection between brains and persons – between Amy, the individual we know and love, and the brain residing within Amy's skull.

Today we also hear about neurotechnological approaches, where neural devices are implanted in the brain to function as a "second brain". Currently this technology is directed towards producing corrective tools for physical disabilities, such as developing microelectrodes for placing in the visual cortex to electrically stimulate the brain to see scenes from a miniature camera (Maguire & McGee, 1999; Mussa-Ivaldi & Miller, 2003). Brain-machine interfaces capable of stimulating the cellular processes for learning and memory could be used as a means of rehabilitation following strokes, especially to bring about muscle activity and the movement of limbs. Other forms of artificial brain prostheses could assist people with memory disorders to regain the ability to store new memories. This could prove very useful in learning to recognise a new face, or remember directions to a new location.

These attempts at therapy are simply extensions of well-known procedures used extensively to improve the functioning of other body organs, such as the heart and gastrointestinal tract, and by themselves appear to pose no threats to the essential nature of what we are as persons. But would it be possible to use cybernetic transplants, where computer chips would be internalised in the brain? In this way, it is suggested that it might prove possible to increase the dynamic range of senses, enabling people to see currently invisible wavelengths, or to enhance memory, or to enable constant access to information where and when it is needed. Such implants might even have a role to play in moral decision-making (see Chapter 7).

Implants of this nature will become part of the individual in question, and will probably change them in some permanent way. In no sense, though, do even these intrusions imperil the close relationship between brain and person. Rather, their ethical and moral acceptability would depend on whether they brought healing and wholeness to the person, whether they assisted that person in relating to God, and whether they improved interpersonal relationships and encouraged all-round fulfilment.

It should now be clear why I categorically dismissed the "brain as a machine" model. As we saw in Chapter 2 when discussing design, the classic view of machines is that they are manufactured according to certain specifications, so that they function in certain predetermined ways. When they cease to function as designed, they are adjusted or repaired so that they again work as required. When I buy a machine I am provided with the specifications of the particular model, and the only expectation I can have is that the model I purchase will do the things I am assured it will do. The human brain is entirely different from this. My brain was not designed to conform to some predetermined pattern. What I am, and what other people recognise as characteristically me, could not have been predicted at the time of my birth – even by some hypothetical super-being who had detailed information about the present and future states of my brain (MacKay, 1988). What they could not have known would have been the numerous environments that would have an impact on my (and my brain's) development, nor could they have known the decisions I would take throughout my life, all of which would influence my brain and my future directions as a person.

Let's work out in a little more detail what this might mean in practice. When a baby is born, that baby's brain is immature. It is nothing like a miniature version of the adult's brain into which it will develop. It will undergo considerable changes as it *becomes* the brain of the adult, many of these changes being totally unknown at birth. For example, Paul 1 moves from one country to another at ten years of age, and then moves to yet a different country at 30. Paul 1 has three siblings, and lives in a very supportive family and community environment. By contrast, imagine an alternative set of circumstances according to which Paul 2 remains in the same location in which he was raised, is an only child, and is raised from the age of five solely by his mother. Even though Paul 1 and Paul 2 started out with identical brains, they will be substantially different people by the age of 40, even if only these few environmental circumstances are taken into consideration. There is no way in which the personalities of either Paul 1 or Paul 2 could be predicted in any detail prospectively.

The *personal model* I am espousing reflects these ongoing interactions between what we are as people, the organisation and plasticity of our brains, every facet of our environment, and all the relationships of which we are a part. The danger is that it might be too easy to modify people's brains and behaviour, with all the immense implications this has for what we are as people. This is where neuroscience could prove to be a catastrophic danger to human well-being.

Before exploring this dimension, it is interesting to reflect that the grave concerns so commonly expressed about developments in genetics (see Chapters 1 and 2) neglect what are probably the far greater issues raised by neuroscience. Inroads into the human person by neuroscience have been available for many years, and one does not have to wait for increasingly sophisticated neuroscientific procedures to come on board. They are with us. Strangely, the postulated allurements of genetic modification seem far more forbidding than the actual threats to personal integrity posed by current neuroscience.

Improving brains

The major drive to improve people's brains comes in the form of psychopharmaceuticals, with the desire to find drugs to combat everything from shyness and forgetfulness, to sleepiness and stress. This is the world of what Arthur Caplan has described as "super-Prozacs" (Caplan, 2002). This also introduces us to the debate on where to draw the line between therapy and enhancement, a debate usually encountered in a theoretical manner in genetics and yet a far more substantial debate in neuroscience (see also Chapter 7).

The issue here is how to distinguish between the *normal* and the *enhanced*. For example, how much depression is normal? While clinical depression is a recognised clinical entity, what are we to make of the low-grade, subclinical depression with which many people live their whole lives? Is there any virtue in living with low-grade depression if it can be obliterated? In other words, what is normal? Similarly, should we treat hyperactivity in children who appear to some to be stretching the bounds of normal behaviour patterns? Does Ritalin administration have a role as part of a genuine therapeutic regime, or is it more at home as a means of social manipulation? What we have here are instances of treading a fine line between the normal and the pathological. But which is which?

Then there is the slight deterioration in memory that accompanies ageing, demonstrated by minor forgetfulness in everyday activities. This is now referred to as *age-associated memory impairment*. Is this normal or abnormal? Should it be viewed as no more than an interesting phenomenon, or is it a mild disease state? If the latter, it may justify treatment with a variety of drugs aimed at modifying the brain's levels of a range of neurotransmitter chemicals, or enzymes that influence key memory transmitter substances. This is an important issue, since mild memory losses may be a prelude to *mild cognitive impairment* and ultimately the dementia of Alzheimer's disease. But, of course, they may not. In the other direction, drugs influencing memory could prove useful in younger age groups, where improvement in test scores at school and university would be the driving force. From this we see all too clearly the shift from normality to disease and back again, driven by a host of powerful factors, from attempts to forestall the dementia in a tragic condition like Alzheimer's disease, to the fears of the affluent world which are well aided and abetted by commercial pressures within the pharmaceutical industry (Arnst, 2003).

How do we determine the boundaries of normality, and how do we know when these are being transgressed? There is no easy answer, since routinely accepted biological limits are wide and the concept of normality is broad. Is the person in question able to function acceptably in society? But even this has limits, because it depends on the nature of the demands placed on individuals by their positions. The concept of normality appears to be more tenuous than frequently assumed.

On top of this there are more grotesque examples. In certain societies Christians have been diagnosed as mentally unstable and in need of psychiatric treatment. This simply serves to show that the murky border between illness and health is a dynamic one, with its own inherent uncertainties. Consequently, the notion of mental and behavioural enhancement is a deeply troubling one, necessitating some very careful manoeuvring. It is relatively easy to argue against enhancements, where the intention is to change people who already fall within the normal range and bestow on them capacities they do not already possess. No matter how unclear normality may be, what we have here is a deliberate move to make acceptably functioning people into something they are not, by modifying their brains.

But what about those who appear to be functioning unacceptably? If the aim of therapies is to cure or prevent diseases that hinder someone from functioning within society, there is a place for the use of brain modifying drugs to bring those people's capacities within normal biological limits. The aim here is to use neuroscience to bring wholeness to people suffering from recognisable diseased states.

Normality and disease

However, care is even required here. The concept of "diseased states" is a malleable one. Consequently, any modification of the brain utilising psychopharmaceuticals or behaviour therapy has to be controlled by the welfare of the people concerned, and not simply to enable them to conform to the mores of society. What is more, people live within communities and societies, and help may consist principally of effecting improvements to the social structures around them. Direct assaults on their brains may be inappropriate. But no matter how we argue these points, perplexing situations remain, where people's actions appear to be unnervingly dominated by the organisation of their brains. Consider these two examples.

When the brains of depressed subjects who have committed suicide are examined, it is invariably found that there is a reduction in one of the brain's neurotransmitters, serotonin. This deficiency can lead to a predisposition to impulsive and aggressive behaviour, suggesting that the individual is at risk of acting on suicidal thoughts. More specifically, this loss of serotonin is mainly found in the pre-fontal cortex (the area situated just above the eyes), and has an important impulse-dampening role. It has even been proposed that the more lethal the suicide attempt, the greater the serotonin deficiency (Ezzell, 2003).

These data can be viewed from different perspectives. One approach is to conclude that individuals with such deficiencies have little way of escaping suicide attempts. However, even many researchers see the situation as being more complex than this, since these serotonin deficits do not exist in isolation, but are found alongside other deficits in the brain. An alternative approach is to search for tools that will help develop tests for individuals who might be at risk from suicide, so that better treatment strategies can be devised. There may be genetic factors, and yet any predisposing gene or genes have so far proved elusive. And we often do not know which comes first – the serotonin deficit or precipitating social factors. The response of someone whose mother had committed suicide is helpful: "These statistics serve as warnings to me and to others with biological ties to suicide ... Perhaps someday science will better understand the basis for such harrowing acts so that families like mine will be spared" (Ezzell, 2003).

The second example is that of homosexuality, where a neurobiological link has been proposed. In the early 1990s the idea was put forward that there is a difference between homosexual and heterosexual men in the structure of a brain region called the hypothalamus (Le Vay, 1991). The research focused on one group of nerve cells within a particular region of the hypothalamus, this group appearing to be larger in heterosexual men. However, this finding by itself fails to provide any useful clues about whether the difference was present at birth, nor about whether it led to the homosexuality or resulted from it (or had nothing at all to do with sexual orientation).

Another difference between homosexual and heterosexual men lay in the size of a bundle of nerve fibres, the anterior commissure, which is a structure that connects right and left regions of the brain (Allen & Gorski, 1992). Exactly the same considerations apply here, since there is no evidence of which came first, nor whether these differences have the least significance behaviourally. Similar comments apply to a number of other studies looking at differences in hormonal levels and stress during pregnancy, and differing abilities of the different groups on visuospatial tasks.

These examples illustrate very clearly the issues at stake. Simple conclusions based on brain features alone are unlikely to be helpful. Decisions concerning the bounds of normality are not decided solely on the basis of biological criteria; they incorporate social, philosophical and theological considerations as well. However, the answer is not to ignore brain differences, by contending that they do not matter; nor should we automatically assume the findings are biased. The neural data form part of a complex overall picture, and constitute an important factor in determining what approaches may be of greatest relevance to people (Jones, 2004a).

As embodied individuals, we all function with clearly discernible boundaries. Regardless of our strengths, we have limitations (biological and social) and weaknesses (towards one addiction or another). If we knew what to look for, we might well find within our brains neural patterns corresponding to these limitations and weaknesses. But we would be foolhardy to conclude that these patterns constitute grounds for relinquishing responsibility for our actions (any more than "spiritual" neural patterns would determine the belief systems and faithfulness of Christians). Responsibility and decision-making are core markers of the human person, even though the personal history of some individuals makes responsible decision-making exceedingly difficult to attain. None of us starts off our lives with a clean genetic or environmental slate, but some people appear to start from a particularly challenging base.

Embodied persons

My emphasis in this chapter has been on both the brain and the person. I have slid between the two, since in my view it is impossible to study the human brain in its many dimensions without appreciating the intimate interrelationship between the brain and the human person. The opposite also holds true. Study of the human person prompts questions galore about the characteristics of the brain at the centre of our bodily existence. We are not human brains with persons attached, any more than we are immaterial persons. This is why I have indulged in two forms of talk: that which stems from what we are as persons, and that which is derived from neuroscience.

We know each other not as brains ensheathed in bodies, but as *embodied persons*. We are people who relate to each other as beings created in the image of God. While neuroscientific descriptions have an essential part to play in this, they elucidate rather than undermine what we are as persons. Knowledge of the brain, of what can go wrong with the brain, and of ways of rectifying deficiencies, should all be welcomed by Christians, since they have the potential to enhance what we are as people before God. Their potential for misuse is as little or as great as in any other human endeavour. Wise discernment and judgement are always called for. For instance, to take Prozac when one is not clinically depressed is to treat it as a cosmetic, but a cosmetic with substantial implications for our view of life. Taking it under these circumstances says far more about our theology and world view than about the state of our brains (Jones, 2004a).

As we saw earlier in this chapter, some distinctions are murky in the extreme: between normality and disease, and hence between treatment and enhancement. On the other hand, one should not conclude from this that there are no distinctions at all. A person suffering from some well-recognised neurological or psychiatric condition may have depressed levels of neurotransmitters in brain regions known to be associated with the impaired functions. Replacement of these neurotransmitters is straightforward therapy, aimed at restoring the individual as an embodied person. Conversely, where there is no evidence of any such imbalance within an individual's brain, provision of these same neurotransmitters is more akin to applying a cosmetic, with consequences ranging from marginally beneficial to clearly deleterious. Either way, it is a lifestyle choice.

I have avoided reference to "the mind", for the reason that I do not find this a helpful concept. When used as a noun, the impression is given that it is an entity of the same type and nature as the brain and existing alongside the brain, with each influencing the other as equivalent but different compartments. Such a notion is foreign to most neuroscientists, who tend to eschew any knowledge or interest in such a concept.

To dismiss the mind like this is not to lapse into materialism, or to deny the existence of mental states. The latter have been implicit in everything I have written, since they are basic to consciousness, self-awareness, and all thought processes. However, they are potentially capable of explanation in physical and chemical terms, not in the sense of explaining away their personal significance, but of providing a physical underpinning to what is occurring when we act in human ways. After all, just as we can explain what happens in the gastrointestinal tract when we eat a satisfying meal, we can explain to some extent what happens in the brain when we make decisions, pray, enjoy fine music, and show acts of love and compassion. Such explanations are just that, explanations; they help us in our understanding of what is taking place. There is no hint of explaining away profound concepts.

Neither have I made reference to "the soul". In no way does this deny a spiritual side to human nature. There is no conflict between the mechanistic explanations of neuroscience and the spiritual emphases of Christians. Neuroscience does not lead inevitably to a materialist stance, with its exclusion of spiritual reality, while spiritual emphases do not demand a role for non-physical influences, such as a soul, on our brains. Just as our mental activity is embodied in our brain activity, so our spiritual awareness and responses are embodied there. Neither mental nor spiritual realities are identical with brain activity, in the sense that they can be understood only in neurological terms. Neither is brain activity any more real than these other realities. They represent different categories, and are to be assessed on their own terms (MacKay, 1987).

By taking seriously our bodies and our brains, we come to appreciate the nature of persons, with their relational core: their relationships with others in the human community and the possibility of relating to God. It is within this context that the brain and an understanding of it through neuroscience has its part to play, in providing a groundwork for making these relationships possible and for helping to rectify what sometimes goes wrong. Such a person-centred model fits comfortably in with a Christian understanding of human existence, and also lives congenially with insights from neuroscience.

Chapter 6

A Possible Future World: Clones and Cyborgs

In this chapter I am allowing myself the luxury (or folly) of looking into the future. I say this because we are not good at predicting the future with any accuracy. This is well illustrated by the brief history of cloning (see Chapter 4), where the serious discussions of 40 years ago turned out to be as misleading as they were helpful. It is for this reason that the cries of those who want a resolution to the ethical, not to mention the theological, issues before scientists are allowed to experiment any further are doomed to failure. At the level of detailed analysis, we do not know with any accuracy what questions will arise before they have arisen at a scientific level. The direction that scientists take is so often determined by the inbuilt rationale of the science itself, and not by the pronouncements of ethicists or theologians. While this is a multifaceted question, the one assertion we can definitely make is that we are notoriously poor at predicting exactly what will turn out to be of scientific value.

This poses many difficulties for ethicists and theologians, who feel they are being left behind and have no role in determining what should and should not be done. I see no way around this, and I am not attempting to rectify this problem in this chapter. I shall keep discussion at a general level, and as far as possible I shall relate present trends to those that may lie around the corner. Can we learn anything from these trends, and how do we respond to them?

Delving into the imagination

Imagine a world many years in the future – 2060, in fact. There is nothing special about this particular year, any more than 1984 or 2001 were special. In fact, as we look back on those two years, we probably think of them as fairly ordinary. And yet, when the novels named after them were written, each in its very different way looked forward to a future when life had taken on totally different dimensions – unknown, unparalleled and grimly strange. These were indeed "brave new worlds". 2060 AD will be no different, and yet it is difficult to believe that it will not be a world of biotechnological control and biomedical manipulation.

> In this society cloning is generally accepted. Of every 1,000 babies born, 20 will be clones. Some people have been cloned because they want offspring who are identical to themselves. These offspring are *ego clones*, who have been produced to resemble someone already in existence. Other clones exist because their parents wanted to avoid having children with a certain genetic defect. These are *medically-justified clones*. Some people have cloned one of their children so that the clone could be a compatible bone marrow donor for a much-needed bone marrow transplantation for an existing child.
>
> Cloning has also been widely used by infertile couples, to enable them to have children. But it hasn't been confined to those in a heterosexual marital relationship. Single women and lesbian couples have employed it to have children of their own. Some gay men, and the occasional single man, have also used it, but they have had to employ women as surrogates. What is amazing is that, by and large, clones are treated as ordinary

members of society. Most are anonymous, just as those conceived by IVF are anonymous.

Before we leave this world of nearly 60 years hence, consider another development. This has nothing to do with clones, but with *cyborgs*. Back in the 20th and even in the early 21st century people used to think of cyborgs as part-human and part-machine: unemotional entities and intimidating creatures, the subjects of films but not of real life. In 2060, though, people have become accustomed to cyborgs.

> They are everywhere. What is disconcerting is that it can be very difficult to distinguish cyborgs from ordinary humans. One is sometimes tempted to think that the most intelligent people around are cyborgs, because so many have had brain implants to improve their intelligence, their empathy, or their eyesight or hearing. But what worries many Christians is that more and more people are having large tracts of the frontal lobes of their brains replaced by artificial devices, to make them more loving and considerate. While the intentions are good, it is impossible to know what is "real". There are also concerns because it is just as easy to remove all emotions as to enhance them.
>
> This is the tip of the iceberg. Most people at some stage of their lives have organs like the heart and kidneys replaced by small artificial devices that fit neatly inside their bodies. They don't have to wait for these organs to malfunction to have them replaced; the implants are said to function better than the natural ones. Legs and joints are routinely replaced by prostheses, and few people over the age of 45 have any of their own natural joints. To varying degrees most people are cyborgs.

These pictures might be far removed from what will actually happen in 2060, but that is not the point. Minor errors are irrelevant for my purpose. What these pictures do tell us is that the world of 2060 will not represent a totally different world from that of our present world in the early 2000s. The origins of all the possibilities I have just imagined are already with us. The brave new world is here, and we are living in it whether we realise it or not.

This world is, of course, not inevitable, and as I have indicated my predictions might be completely wrong. Priorities that appear eminently reasonable today might soon be seen to be irrelevant or even obstructionist. The directions charted by committees might emerge as unhelpful and might fail to reflect the most promising avenues for science. This makes charting scientific progress an unenviable task.

It is no wonder, then, that the task of looking many years into the future is a precarious one. I am very aware of this, and I claim no prescience for my own meanderings. Human clones might never be found within most societies (perhaps *any* society), and hence the first part of my 2060 scenario might be very wide of the mark. Most will hope that it is. But let us pretend that clones will exist, and will walk our streets and perhaps even the corridors of power. What then? Will that demonstrate that the scientific possibilities with which I have been dealing are fraught with horrendous problems and aberrant possibilities that we should resist with all our might? This is where such scenarios become relevant for our thinking today. If work currently being undertaken in innocuous looking laboratories will lead inexorably to a world beyond our comprehension, even an unrecognisable world, the implications for how we respond today are enormous.

Very many people see cloning in grim, even nightmarish, terms. It has been compared with the holocaust, and with the tragic excesses of the gas chambers and the horrific experimentation undertaken on innocent subjects. It appears that nothing could be worse, as soulless subhumans roam our streets creating social mayhem. Perhaps less extreme are the claims that they will be the objects of our manipulation and products of our will; in other words, our playthings, our toys, little more than the characters of devilish computerised games.

While the dangers of cloning are widely recognised and are of deep concern to many people, the dangers of cyborgs are far less well recognised. What is fascinating about cyborgs is that, on the one hand, they give the impression of being far more futuristic than clones, and yet on the other they are far closer to us than we realise. This is because the intrusion of the artificial into human life has crept up on us, and is widely accepted. After all, where is the vehement ethical debate about the use of artificial hips or knees? There may be debate about resource issues surrounding their availability, but not about their acceptability for our view of the integrity of the human body. And yet the use of artificial devices in various organs, including the brain, may prove far more radical when used in a widespread fashion across whole populations than would the existence of a limited number of human clones.

In making these statements I am not supporting developments that might usher in either human clones or extreme versions of cyborgs. I am simply reflecting on present attitudes that might lead us in unexpected and perhaps unwanted directions.

The muddled world of cloning

> [Ian Wilmut] was the first man to create fully formed life from adult body parts since Mary Shelley's mad scientist ... Not since God took Adam's rib and fashioned a helpmate for him has anything so fantastic occurred. (*Time* magazine, 1997)

Man has become a creator rivalling only God. (*Time* magazine, 1997)

The difficulty with so much of the talk about cloning is that one is normally provided with pictures of a large number of identical cherubic babies, or a whole lot of Tony Blairs or George W. Bushes, or ordinary middle-class drones. All this is totally misleading, because the pictures routinely shown are of people in the same generation, both the originators and their resulting clones. This is not what cloning will lead to. If I were to be cloned, you wouldn't end up with someone just like me. I wouldn't have an identical twin living around the corner, let alone ten or 20 identical "me's". What you would have would be someone very similar to me but many years younger than me – not too far removed from a very similar son living in another generation (Jones, 2001, 2002).

But why would anyone want to clone or be cloned? This is the most perplexing question of all, and a number of predominant answers are given (in addition to those alluded to in Chapter 2).

To attain immortality

At one extreme, there are those who seem to think so highly of themselves that they must ensure that they continue into the next generation. This is "ego cloning"; cloning for purely egotistical and selfish reasons.

A slight extension of this is to view cloning as a means of cheating death. This, of course, is foolhardy, for the simple reason that a person's clone will be a different person from them. An individual will live on in his or her clone only to the extent that we currently live on in our naturally conceived children. My clone would not be "me" in a more substantial sense than a son or daughter of mine is me. Whatever characteristics they have in common with me are nothing more than that. The person they are and the person I am are not the same. This is an obvious truth: there is no way to cheat death, cloning or no cloning.

A strange extension of this is exhibited by those who have religious reasons for cloning, such as members of the Raelian cult. They believe that humans were created by an extraterrestrial race in their own image, and that Jesus was resurrected through a cloning technique. For them, eternal life can be reached through cloning, and their company Clonaid was established to do precisely this. If cloning people is equivalent to attaining eternal life, it is an entirely different notion of eternal life from any Christian notion. The false claims made repeatedly by the Raelians regarding having actually cloned babies leads one to suspect that none of their claims, either biological or theological, should be taken with any degree of seriousness.

To have genetically related children
A prominent reason for cloning would be the desire of infertile couples to have genetically related children, that is, to have a child genetically related to one of the partners. Or think of a couple in which one partner has a genetic defect; this couple could avoid the risk of passing on this defect to their children by having cloned children of the healthy partner. While these in no way justify cloning, they are probably the most defensible reasons for it, since a child is wanted for its own sake and not to resemble any existing person.

To replace a dead child
Another reason for cloning is to replace a dead baby or a child killed in an accident. And then what about:

- parents looking for a sibling to be a compatible tissue or organ donor for a child dying from leukemia or kidney failure;
- a wife whose husband is dying and who wishes to have biological offspring of the dying husband?

The problem in these cases is that a child is being brought into the world to serve the interests of someone else. And so we have to ask: are these children being loved primarily for their usefulness, rather than for what they bring to the world as unique individuals? This would not be inevitable, but it would be a strong possibility. While some of these cases are heart-rending, we all have to cope with suffering and loss, and a biological solution may be deeply flawed.

Why are people so fearful of cloning?

> Is there a hidden fear that [through cloning] we would be forcing God to give us another soul, thereby bending God to our will, or, worse yet, that we would be creating soul-less beings that were merely genetic shells of humans? (Gina Kolata, 1998)

> We are repelled by the prospect of cloning human beings ... because we feel the violation of things that we rightfully hold dear. We must not transgress what is unspeakably profound. (Leon Kass, 1998)

For many people, the cloning of another human being is so horrific and barbaric that it should be outlawed and made a major criminal offence. Why is there such an abhorrence of cloning?

Human beings should never be altered

Many people think that the innermost workings of what we are as human beings are sacrosanct and should always remain so. In some indefinable way, this central part of us is divine and should not be touched. Cloning is feared because it is thought that it would intrude into this divine centre of our humanity. By producing children with all the characteristics of just one parent rather than the usual two, we will have altered what they are as human beings.

Some Christians are concerned because they wonder whether clones will have souls. For them, cloning is interfering with God's way of making children, and this is wrong. It is a way of designing children, of altering them in ways we think appropriate, and not accepting what God has provided (see Chapter 2).

In the end, whatever we may think of cloning, it seems to me that a clone will be remarkably similar to all of us. Not only this: children who have been cloned would probably surprise us just as ordinary fertilised children surprise us all the time. We have already seen that cloning would be a very crude way of designing human beings, since the clone will be the same as a pre-existing person. If one really wanted to design one's children there are many more efficient ways of doing so that have nothing to do with cloning or even with biology.

Producing humans to order

One of the fundamental fears is that by cloning others we would be mass-producing humans just as one mass-produces cars or washing machines, in that we would be creating humans with predetermined genetic characteristics. The resulting clones would function as we want them to function, do what we want them to do, and believe what we want them to believe. If anything like this were to happen, the critics of cloning would be correct, since it is essential that we can make our own way in the world, that we are free to think in our own ways, and that we can be ourselves.

If clones did lose this freedom, there is no question that they would have been dehumanised. But is this inevitable? I very much doubt that it is, because it would depend in the end on why someone was cloned in the first place and also on the way in which they were raised as children. To get a child to behave exactly as we want them to behave means denying them their freedom, and this has nothing to do with biological cloning. It depends far more on what I call *behavioural cloning*, and, unfortunately, this is something that happens all the time even now in some families and in some societies.

And it is this that should make us ponder. Do we currently allow children the freedom to develop into what they might become? This is an educational question, because it arises repeatedly in work situations. Take universities and postgraduate students. How easy it is to expect a thesis by one of these students to reflect exactly what the supervisor thinks, even down to the exact words used. This is not an isolated phenomenon, and yet it is nothing other than *educational cloning*. Surely students have to mature and make their own way in the world, to become what they can be and not simply reflect the whims and fancies of their supervisors?

Cloning robs people of their genetic uniqueness

If there is one objection that stands out above all others, it is that clones will not be genetically unique. They will have the same genetic constitution as their mother or father. The deep concern here is that clones will lose their uniqueness as human beings, and so will be deprived of their human dignity (see the discussion in Chapter 2).

However, identical twins demonstrate very clearly that

people who are not genetically unique are still unique people. This is hardly surprising, since, as we saw previously, they have different brains. Identical twins *and* clones, should they ever exist, are unique individuals, with different thought processes and ethical responsibility; they would all have to make choices and create their own worlds. They would both have the opportunity of following Christ, and of responding to him. They would be viewed by God as once-and-for-all people, with a dignity and worth that stem from the very high valuation placed upon them by God.

What would be important is that other people did not force them to perform in particular ways. The major problem is always the same: the demands by others to be exactly as these others expect, and therefore to behave in ways acceptable to these other people. This is the best way of ensuring that the freedom of the next generation is stifled and thwarted, and it is always a tragedy, quite apart from issues of cloning.

This is always the problem with group pressure, and conforming to the standards and expectations of those in the group, whether this be a gentlemen's club, a church, or a political party. There has to be room for healthy dissent within the broad parameters of the particular group. Only in this way will new paths be forged, new ideas enunciated, and original thinking explored. Cloning could indeed pose a problem, but unfortunately this would hardly be an entirely new problem.

Clones will be manufactured
This is an objection raised mainly by those Christians who draw a crucial distinction between "begetting" and "making". "Begetting" is normal sexual reproduction, whereas "making" is any form of artificial reproduction. For these writers, "begetting" results in the birth of someone like us, whereas

"making" results in the birth of someone unlike us. They argue that we can love only children who have been begotten, whereas those who have been made are less than us and will be used by us. This has always struck me as being grossly unfair on those parents who have had children by IVF, and who love them deeply and always do their best for them.

Essentially this is an argument against any form of technological interference with the reproductive process, which some view as a move away from the personal towards the impersonal. They want to retain the idea that children are a gift from God, to be accepted for what they are. I have great sympathy with this, but it is an argument against any form of artificial reproduction and against any medical intervention in the reproductive process. I see no reason why children cannot be accepted as a gift from God even when there has been some technical and medical assistance. After all, we do this in all other areas, when we thank God for the work of health professionals in bringing about healing and a return to wholeness.

Is an individual with an artificial hip or someone else's heart less human than an individual with their own hip and heart? Surely, the answer has to be "no", unless there is discrimination against those with artificial parts or transplanted organs. And then it is the discrimination that is the problem, and not the reconstructed body parts.

Should we clone?

Under no circumstances should we contemplate cloning other humans at present. The enormous risks currently associated with attempting to clone laboratory and farm animals tell us that cloning would be incredibly dangerous. In no way can one even attempt to justify the procedure in humans, either now or in the foreseeable future. At present, the chasm of unknowns is prodigious, and no one acting in an ethical manner would even contemplate cloning humans. The overall success rate is of the order of 1–2% of cloned embryos producing live births. Of those animals born alive, many of them have abnormalities of one sort or another.

Of course, this argument is in no way unique to cloning. It is a pragmatic argument, and the same applies to any other scientific or clinical development. This may change with time, but that will depend on a large amount of animal experimentation and a considerable increase in understanding of the scientific processes involved. Many other arguments against cloning also tend to be pragmatic ones, notably psychological ill effects resulting from identity confusion or from the notoriety attached to being a clone. These ill effects may or may not follow, but it is appropriate that attention is drawn to them. Nevertheless, all new procedures have unknowns attached to them, their seriousness requiring assessment in their own right.

Still, many writers regard cloning as fundamentally different from any other process, even in the reproductive area. They may be right. It is on these grounds that there is such widespread agreement on the need to ban all cloning of human individuals. I find myself in an ambivalent position, since while I have no desire to promulgate the cloning of individuals, I remain suspicious of the shallowness of so many of the arguments against it (Jones, 2002b). Admittedly, there would be exceedingly few therapeutic reasons to justify using it, even if it were legal. And so it remains something of an uneasy conundrum, on which very large numbers of words have been expended, unlike the situation of cyborgs.

From cyborgs to cyberspace

Cyborgs are generally viewed as fitting far more into the world of science fiction than do clones, and so people are not as fearful of what they might mean for us. To me, this is a short-sighted response, since it shows we are unaware of how much the artificial already intrudes into our lives. The intrusion of greatest relevance to cyborgs is cyberspace – the Internet and all that goes with it. This is something that has overtaken most, if not all, of us in a remarkably short time.

It is a truism to state that we now know a great deal of what it means to be linked almost effortlessly to people in every part of the world. More and more of our business transactions are dependent on use of the Internet, and even ordinary life now incorporates these linkages in the way in which letters and telephones did a very short time ago. The advantages at every level of society are obvious, and the disadvantages appear to revolve around the misuse of this technology, with its spam, its viruses, and undue ease of access to illicit and harmful activities. All this is true, and yet all too readily its major ramifications for our privacy, and even for what we are as people, remain little more than dim shadows in the background.

Technological developments always have repercussions for the way in which we think of our existence (Board for Social Responsibility, 1999). Ships, railways, cars and planes transformed our sense of geography and travel. They dramatically changed our sense of distance, enabling us to relate to those in distant lands and cities in ways previously unimaginable. This, in turn, altered our *relationships* with others. It enabled us to go to places we would never have contemplated, and in this way made us part of a worldwide community. This was enhanced by other transformations in communication, epitomised by the emergence of efficient telephone systems.

What is fascinating about changes like these is that they don't just affect our ability to communicate with others. They actually have profound effects on us, on the sort of people we are. In other words, these changes don't remain external to us, simply improving our quality of life. They transform the way in which we think, since they alter what we think is possible, and therefore the character of our expectations. We are no longer prepared to live as people lived 100 years ago, let alone 1,000 years ago. We are all modern people, in the sense that every one of us has been moulded by everyday technology. We think differently from pre-moderns, and while these brief comments have only touched on travel and communication, the differences are perhaps even more profound in medicine and health.

We no longer expect most of our children to die before the age of five years, and we don't ourselves expect to die before the age of 50 years. We don't expect to have to have ten children in order for just one or two to survive to adulthood. Indeed the death of children is now regarded as a tragedy, because it is relatively rare and is deemed to be out of the ordinary. This means that ordinary people are far more removed from death and its reality in their immediate surroundings than people were 100 years ago and are today in many countries in the two-thirds world. While we do not usually decry the human control that makes these developments reality, since they are generally viewed as exemplary, they have had dramatic repercussions for ordinary existence, and for the way in which human life is evaluated. This, in turn, has clear theological implications for our view of God's providence and intervention in human affairs.

But what about *cyberspace*? The nature of this new form of communication and the ease of access to almost limitless information have profoundly affected our place in time and space. We are beginning to see ourselves differently, and have accepted a new way of relating to others, a way that depends far less on face-to-face encounter and far more on "virtual" contact. In some cases virtual reality is becoming of greater importance than actual reality, and this could have considerable repercussions for the meaning we place on actual people.

The implications of these thoughts are vast, affecting everything we touch: from what we eat to how we reproduce, from the manner in which we communicate to the illnesses we expect to avoid. The salutary reflection is that these changes are almost inevitable. Not many people like to admit this, since they think they can determine what is allowed in and what is excluded. This is probably an illusion.

It was this realisation that, over many years and well before the advent of cyberspace, led some writers to express grave reservations about modern technology. Two examples within the Christian sphere were Karl Barth (1961) and Jacques Ellul (1964). Barth's concern was with the human lust for power, and with the possibility of it becoming a technique of disorder and destruction. Ellul concentrated on technique's drive for efficiency and its dependence upon rational conscious activity. This led him to conclude that technology has developed independently of any human control, resulting in the construction of an artificial universe that constrains and enslaves human beings.

Should we fear a computerised world?

As we turn our attention more specifically to computers and cyberspace, and even to cyborgs in the future, a number of features emerge as of central importance (Board for Social Responsibility, 1999).

The first is that the use of computers is *pervasive*. They are now integral components of so much on which our lives depend. We are all touched by them, even when we are blissfully unaware of their presence. Our culture can no longer exist without them.

Second, computers transcend familiar physical limits. The old physical boundaries with which we are all familiar are ceasing to exist in cyberspace. As a result, computers are making a *qualitative change* to the way we live. Doing away with these boundaries affects our relationships with one another, and therefore our social fabric. This is the essence of what I have referred to as "the death of distance", since it makes possible new relationships and communities, ones which wouldn't exist in the absence of computers.

Third, computers affect the *way in which we think of ourselves*, and even what we regard as real. As we create an increasing array of virtual-reality worlds, the effect is to blur the boundary between people and machines. This is what cyborgs are meant to do, but this is already happening. As computers become increasingly minute and ever faster, this trend will almost inevitably intensify. In other words, we are fast entering the sphere of cyborgs, and we are dimly beginning to realise that the cyborgs are actually ordinary people like us. They are not a select group of entities brought into being by technocrats as experimental models of some future race; they are you and me, who appear to be craving for a cyborgian (to create a new term) world.

What we are encountering here is a principle I touched upon in Chapters 1 and 2, namely, that developments are gradual and that the decisions to adopt new procedures are generally taken by the population at large. True, the developments themselves are brought about by scientists and technocrats, but once available they are seized upon by ordinary people. They appear to meet some felt need.

These are interesting observations, which force us to ask a number of fundamental questions (Board for Social Responsibility, 1999):

- What is true?
- What are real relationships?
- Who are our neighbours?
- How is privacy to be protected?
- How do we judge the reliability of the vast amount of information available?
- Where does power lie?
- What is a person?
- How are humans different from computers?
- What place might computers have in enhancing our lives as humans?

While I have no intention of exploring these detailed areas or of attempting to answer these questions, what shines through are their theological and philosophical connotations. No matter how we answer these questions, we cannot escape having to confront very basic questions about the meaning of life and relationships, how we are to treat others, and what makes us the people we are.

The questions themselves will take us in different directions, and any one new development might satisfy us on some counts but not on others. In other words, as with practically all the technological possibilities we are encountering in these pages, we are not generally faced with a simple good/bad dichotomy. Judgement and wisdom are prerequisites for assessing and weighing up where we are to go, what is of value and what is dross.

Clough (2002), in his analysis of cyberspace, is acutely aware that this technology has the potential to dominate rather than to serve us. While appreciating the excitement of what it has to offer, he balances grand utopian visions with its threat to treat human beings as little more than machines. He is also cautious about what he regards as its temptation to think there are places where we can hide from each other and escape from our responsibility to identify with real people.

In view of what I have just been describing, it is surprising that there isn't far more discussion about this intrusion into our lives. Why aren't we as worried about cyberspace as we are about clones? The trouble is that we have gratefully accepted the increasing convenience cyberspace brings to us, without thinking about its longer-term implications. As with any other development like this, cyberspace and our increasing dependence on technology are mixed blessings. They have positive and negative aspects, but at present we are so intrigued by the positive that we haven't even begun to think seriously about the negative. This is not an argument against cyberspace or against the cyborgs of the future. But it is a warning that we are always to judge what such a development has to offer.

Currently, computers are usually external to our bodies, but even as external appendages they have enormous implications for what we are as people. What, then, can we expect when they become internal – implants in various organs, especially in our brains? Our partnership with computers today is far more pervasive than most realise, since our use of them leaves data shadows; they "remember" us in a way in which a photocopier doesn't. In other words, even now our partnership with computers is a symbiotic one (Board for Social Responsibility, 1999).

However, once they have been internalised, a new world of cybernetic transplants will be upon us. Instead of transplanting organs from other people or biological tissue from others, computer chips could be transplanted. This might be done in order to rectify something that has gone wrong or to enhance performance in a certain area. When implanted within someone, they will become part of that person, and will probably permanently change them (see also Chapter 5). The effects, of course, will depend on where they are implanted and for what purpose.

It is impossible to know how far down this path these or similar developments will take us, and rampant speculation may be idle. However, could the day come when there will be direct interaction between internalised computers in our brains and a person's neural processes and decision-making? After all, our brains are physical objects and, as we saw in Chapter 5, are amenable to modification and manipulation. Would the involvement of computers in moral decision-making be mainly a threat or a benefit?

Strange as these issues may sound, they are not unique to computers. As with any form of manipulation, we need to ask whether they will:

- be used for therapeutic or dubious enhancement purposes;
- alter the personality of the person concerned, either for good or for bad;
- allow one person to control another, thereby contributing to injustice and exploitation;
- be used to enhance quality of life, by allowing people to fulfil themselves;
- improve or detract from human relationships;
- assist or hinder a person's relationship with God;
- diminish or accentuate the divide between the privileged and the underprivileged;
- be used for the common good or for devious purposes.

Each of these is a judgement call, and each demands moral and spiritual discernment. How, then, can we tackle some of these issues, using Christian directives?

What can clones and cyborgs teach us?

If we were to walk out of of our home or office and be confronted by either a clone or a cyborg, how should we treat them? Many people have pictured them as being produced to carry out menial tasks or dangerous work. Pictures like this are grotesque, for the simple reason that they will be people just like you and me. Once in existence they will soon emerge as being people who have been created by God; they will have the gift of human life, and they will have a God-bestowed dignity. God will love them as much as he loves us.

It's interesting that Jesus repeatedly emphasised the central place of the *weak and disadvantaged in society* – those unable to defend themselves or stand up for themselves (Matthew 19:13–15; Luke 18:15–17; James 1:26–27). And so he placed the spotlight on children, on widows, on the outcasts and on the unlovely. These were not to be kicked around as of no significance; neither were they to be treated as of lesser value than the powerful and the power brokers of their society. All are equal under God and all must be treated as equal.

Clones and cyborgs will have major effects on society only if they are created simply to do their masters' wills. But this can be accomplished only by treating them as less than human, something we have been extremely good at through the centuries.

We are all made in the image of God, however we came into being – whether we were born into riches or into poverty, whether we were wanted or unwanted, whether we were fertilised naturally or artificially, and even in the future if we were to be cloned or partly artificial.

It's all too easy to treat some people or some groups of people as subhuman or at least as somewhat lower than everyone else. Unfortunately, we do this all the time, and it's these attitudes that lead to the biggest problems facing us in our world. And yet whenever we do this, we are judging people as of little worth, something that God never does (Jones, 2001).

This was very well brought out in the film *Gattaca*, which was set in a world of very sophisticated genetic technology. The major problems there were with social attitudes, since those who were apparently second rate on a genetic scale of values were treated as second rate by that society. The end result was that a form of genetic determinism ruled the society, and inequality was rampant. What was fascinating about the film was that certain individuals, who were the "invalids", the second-rate citizens, refused to accept their lowly status and subtly demonstrated that they were more than their genes. This is a profoundly Christian emphasis, which points to the importance of wholeness and integrity in our lives, since these mirror what we are in the sight of God.

Clones and cyborgs teach us the value of *diversity*, the value of people who are different from us. And so, if we were to be confronted by a clone or a cyborg, our response should be exactly as it would be to anyone else: and that is acceptance and a recognition of who they are before God. Christians believe that we are all one in Christ Jesus; there is neither Jew nor Greek, there is neither slave nor free, there is neither male nor female (Galatians 3:26–29), and we can add there is neither black nor white, Asian nor Caucasian, clone nor fertilised, natural nor artificial.

But we only accept people's diversity when we also accept that we are to serve them, regardless of how they were conceived or subsequently modified. We are never to bring others into the world so that they can dance to our tune, and this includes perfectly ordinary and straightforward children, as well as clones. Cloning, therefore, is not a quick way to the production of a servant class. And cyborgs are not a quick way to either efficiency or slavery.

The artificial and the natural

The trouble with the vision presented by cyborgs is that it tempts people to think that the artificial is always superior to the natural. It also tempts us to think that what we have now is not good enough. It can be improved on, and there is something better to look forward to. But this something better is something we manufacture, something we make, something we can touch and feel. This is not to deny that artificial prostheses can be of enormous value to many people, but by themselves they do not impart meaning to human existence. They are valuable therapeutic tools, and we are to be immensely grateful for them. But this is the context within which their contribution to our lives is to be seen and assessed.

Cyberspace provides enhanced communication, but this is of little use if we have nothing to communicate. What are essential are relationships and values, which come from neither technology nor cyberspace. This is where a Christian vision is needed to impart purpose and meaning, and provide a framework for all our endeavours in these fascinating and demanding areas.

One of the problems with modern science and modern technology is that we take ourselves too seriously. We are unable to laugh at ourselves in the way in which clowns laugh at themselves and at others. We think we can accomplish more than we really can, and that we actually do hold the world in our hands. All too readily we come to think of ourselves as omnipotent, able to bring perfect life into being, able to bring to an end imperfect life, and able to ward off death indefinitely. All these are dangerous illusions (Jones, 2001).

No matter how great our abilities, they need to be balanced by *humility*. Only in this way will they be directed towards improving the welfare of as many people as possible (Matthew 23:8–12,23–26). We are not the centre of all wisdom, and we need to laugh at our overweening pretensions and misguided designs. Whenever we think we can "cure" death, or create babies in our image, we need to step back and laugh at the comic situation created by our pretensions.

To think that cloning is the path into some bright new future for the human race is to misunderstand the science of cloning. We need to laugh at our futile and misguided pretensions. Humour, and awareness that we are accountable to God, will prevent us from making fools of ourselves. Nevertheless, there may be some important therapeutic applications of the cloning of tissues. Even here, though, humour has its place. Not everyone will be able to have their own tissue banks. Even if they could, tissue banks are no panacea for every illness, let alone for disillusionment, dashed expectations, spoiled relationships, or a lack of hope and fulfilment.

Chapter 7

Repairing and Manipulating People: Medicine Too Far?

The previous chapters should have demonstrated as clearly as anything could that our world has changed out of all recognition from what it was a mere 20–30 years ago. This applies across all fields of human endeavour, including of course the one which is the focus of my attention, that of modern biomedicine. There is no escaping the all-pervasive tentacles of genetic possibilities, the emergence of forms of treatment applied at the embryonic stage, and the increasing attractions offered by using embryos to benefit others within the human community. Increasingly sophisticated and precise technological forms of therapy abound, particularly neuroscientific ones, inherent within which are degrees of control and manipulation novel to the human race.

Previously unimagined levels of control and manipulation are required to make developments of this nature possible. These, in turn, pose theological as well as ethical and scientific challenges. This is because human beings are the manipulators and the manipulated. For many Christians, the tension inherent within this dichotomy is an exceedingly uneasy one. On the one hand it points to technologies that appear to be bestowing on humans a burgeoning control over themselves and others, and yet on the other hand we get the profound feeling that this is threatening God's control. Should this creeping control by humans be stopped before we usurp realms rightly left exclusively to God? Indeed, do such God-only realms exist?

A manipulated community

In order to illustrate some of the issues raised by technological manipulation, let us consider a hypothetical community existing well into the 21st century, a community akin to the one in Chapter 6.

> In this community technology has become indispensable for all human activities. Forty per cent of babies are born as a result of some form of artificial fertilisation; the use of artificial organs is commonplace, although pig organs are still quite commonly used for transplantation purposes; the use of animal and human cloning for therapeutic purposes is routine, and a small number of cloned individuals are found in most towns (although you would have no idea who they are). Tissue transplantation to alleviate the worst effects of Alzheimer's disease is regarded as normal, and some familial forms of the disease are prevented by genetic manipulation. Parkinson's disease can be cured in its early stages by neurotransmitter chips implanted in patients' brains. Genetic enhancement is successful in eliminating some personality traits, so that rage and anger can be "removed" during gestation. This community is also a cyberspace community, where virtual worlds have transformed the nature of time and place, everyone is instantly accessible, and yet face-to-face human relationships have largely disappeared. It is becoming a lonely community.

The people of this manipulated community expect technological "fixes" for almost everything. And yet even they realise that these fixes do not solve all their problems. Nevertheless, every new piece of technology that becomes available will be developed. The future is as uncertain as it ever was, and the technology can let them down; it goes wrong from time to time, and on occasion the results are not what was anticipated. Sometimes there are even tragedies. And, in the end, everyone withers and dies, although some of them rebel against death far more than they would have done 50 years previously. Death is far more of an ugly intrusion than it used to be. This community is, of course, the world we inhabit, or will do shortly. It may be a strange world, but it's *our* world.

What is depicted in this scenario is the tension between the power and the limitations of technology. Human beings need more than a technological diet to find fulfilment as persons in community. On the other hand, humans are far from fixed biologically. Consequently, considerable care is needed to ensure that we do not rush to premature conclusions, without first assessing the theological parameters within which we are working. Let us first turn to these.

Some theological parameters

One of the fundamental tenets of Christian theology is that humans are created in the image and likeness of God. It is this that is seen as distinguishing human beings from all other creatures and plants (Genesis 1:26–31, 9:6). There is something special about humans, and this is one way of expressing it. The concept of the image of God has been interpreted in a variety of ways historically. It can refer to the spirituality, rationality and morality of human beings, to their dominion over creation, to their capacity to enter into relationship both with God and with other humans in human community, and to physical attributes such as their physical bodies and upright posture. It is these capacities taken together that in Christian thinking bestow upon humans their uniqueness.

The phrase "image of God" points towards God as the original, and in certain respects to human beings as copies of that original (Genesis 1:26–31, 9:1–7; 1 Corinthians 11:7; 2 Corinthians 4:4; Colossians 1:15; James 3:9). We imitate God by acting as he acts. Human beings have many Godlike attributes; we are persons; we make choices and act on them; we have values and value systems; we are aware of ourselves and of others; and we are held responsible for our actions. Implicit within these concepts is the moral agency of human beings, in that God treats us as people capable of deciding issues morally and rationally (Genesis 2:16–17). The moral responsibility characteristic of humans is an echo of the moral responsibility of God, enshrining as it does the capacity to act wisely and in love. Consequently, we have a mandate to heal and restore God's creation (Jones, 1999).

This is demonstrated by the disobedience of humans, as much as by their obedience. The dramatic depiction of the former in the portrait of Adam and Eve in the Garden of Eden (Genesis 3:1–19) only underlines the high expectations that God has of human beings. The new community established in Christ is based on the premise that members of this community will be transformed into the image of Christ, who perfectly reflects God (Romans 8:29; 2 Corinthians 3:18; Colossians 3:10).

A traditional understanding of this theme is that of humans as stewards (Genesis 2:15; Luke 12:42–48, 16:1–13; 1 Corinthians 4:1–2), who act in a responsible fashion in all areas of their lives, including the conservation and protection of what God has created. God designed the universe according to a plan, and the task of humans is to remain faithful to this plan. While this understanding is a conservative one, the task of being a steward of God's creation is transformative. There may be God-ordained limits and boundaries, but attempts to bring about healing and wholeness can be far-reaching. This is because an essential facet of acting in this manner is human creativity, mirroring as it does God's creativity.

In this conservative interpretation the emphasis is on *therapy*, at the heart of which lie attempts to rectify what has gone wrong and to restore people and the ecosphere to a functioning state. And so we are to restore the world, rather than accept it and its fallen state in some fatalistic manner. We are to understand, protect, care for, develop, nurture and manage the earth for God and ourselves. We are to change the world for good, although, as is only too obvious, self-centred changes can be detrimental and can work against the interests of others. Nevertheless, in spite of incipient dangers, God does not readily abrogate human freedom. Decision-making is central to human life, and is both a privilege and a responsibility. But the immensity of this responsibility is held in check by a further consideration, and this is that God is to be placed firmly at the centre of human existence (Jones, 2002a).

The dangers are immense, since God is readily replaced by technological achievement and human prowess (see Chapter 6). Alternatively, human freedom can be limited by imposing arbitrary rules and regulations. Both lead to the same end point: the loss of an elevated view of human dignity, and the loss of God-bestowed freedom.

Although I have branded this traditional interpretation a conservative one, it is only conservative in a broad sense. If followed through it allows the use of many creative therapeutic ventures as long as their bottom line is the attainment of wholeness. The use of artificial devices, means of bypassing normal functioning, and many forms of experimentation can all be accommodated under this umbrella. What is important is the welfare of the patient, the person being treated, not the maintenance of some unchanging and rigidly defined norm. It is unfortunate that much of the opposition to current biotechnology that ventures from within Christian circles fails to appreciate the potentially transformative power of human creativity as a manifestation of our creation in God's own image.

But is the extent of human creativity greater than I have just outlined? Does it incorporate the mandate to go beyond preserving what God has already created, and participate in what may be described as additional acts of creation? It is in this sense that humans are sometimes referred to as being co-creators with God; the created co-creator (Hefner, 1989; Peters, 2003a). This term underscores the fact that God creates differently from any form of creating of which humans are capable, while humans have themselves been created by God and hence are creatures. In addition it signifies that creation does not stand still, and humans have some influence on the direction it takes (Peters, 2003a). Peters provocatively states that:

> We are condemned to be creative. We cannot avoid it. Our ethical mandate, then, has to do with the purposes toward which our creativity is directed and the degree of zeal with which we approach our creative tasks. (Peters, 2003a, p. 16)

The emphasis here is on humans as co-workers with God, because human work is needed if God's full purposes in the universe are to be realised. Theoretically, this is a much-expanded view of human intervention in the world, since the world is still a work in progress, the fulfilment of which is partially dependent on our interacting with it through the creative use of our freedom. One controversial possibility here is that humans might actually be in a position to mitigate some of the effects of the Fall and so in some measure improve human and planetary life. Coupled with this is the possibility of enhancement as a fundamental scientific and social thrust.

It is not my task to argue the respective merits of these particular theological interpretations. What I would say is that, from my more pragmatic stance, I doubt whether they lead to substantially different positions in practice. I have already emphasised what I regard as the breadth of a thera-peutically-based approach, and I have no problem in envisaging that this accommodates procedures such as IVF for infertility, somatic-cell gene therapy, neural grafting, and even pre-symptomatic interventions at the embryonic stage to alleviate or bypass major diseases. Outlining a list like this is not automatic justification for any of these procedures; it is simply an affirmation that they can all be governed by a ther-apeutic rationale.

While debates galore have been conducted on the respec-tive merits of therapy and enhancement, or more specifically on the dangers of enhancement, my emphasis has been on therapy. I am unable to discern what enhancement might mean in realistic terms, since the scenarios usually envisaged are so far from reality as to be unhelpful. Additionally, as I have just indicated, the boundaries of therapy are extensive, going well beyond what is frequently envisaged for it. In other words, the distinction between therapy and enhancement might be less hard and fast than generally imagined (see Chapter 2). Therapy is not simply an adherence to the status quo, but is an exploration of the possibilities opened up by technologies and new approaches that might benefit patients and the community at large.

As we have seen, the one theological thrust that should not be downplayed is *creativity*, which emerges as of profound significance for every area of human life, from the arts to sci-ence and commerce, and yet its thrust is to break down old barriers, to explore unexplored territory, and to establish new frontiers for investigation and development. But, in the end, what is crucial is the welfare of the individuals concerned, and of as many within the community as possible. The determining question is always to be: what will uphold human dignity and human value – both now and in the future?

Although I have concentrated on creation, and humans as creators under God, we should not ignore the complementary Christian doctrines of redemption and eschatology. Together they provide a window into the future, indicating the importance of being open to God's future, and seeking to determine how God's new creation might impact on our present moral responsibilities. These provide a future-directed context for all we do in medicine, including our responsibility for future generations and making us aware of the impact of our actions and decisions on those who will come after us (Peters, 2003b).

The transformative power of medical intervention

Against this background, let us look back through human history, where we can find numerous examples of intrusions into nature. These have taken many forms: building houses to protect people from the weather; draining swamps infested with malaria-bearing mosquitoes; undertaking surgery; and using antibiotics. Time and again, the Christian church has been behind these ventures, with its investment in hospitals and clinics, and its efforts to make communities self-sufficient with adequate clean water supplies. When confronted by diseases such as diabetes, heart disease and colon cancer, individuals and societies have done their best to combat them with the most effective weapons at their disposal, even though it is now obvious that some of them have a genetic component. Medicine has traditionally done its best to cope with these conditions, and the concern normally expressed has not been whether the intrusion is justified, but whether it will enhance or diminish the human condition. This has generally been regarded as an outworking of the Christian emphasis on caring for people and restoring them in body and mind.

The improvements are all illustrations of biomedical manipulation, even though some have been technologically unsophisticated. But, in spite of what I have written, have these efforts been misguided, and have they conformed to Christian goals? If we had our time over again, would we go in these directions? Perhaps we should have stopped in 1850 or 1900 or 1950; perhaps the Christian church at those times should have called for a moratorium on further developments in anaesthesia or antibiotics or clean water supplies. Even raising the possibility of stopping sounds very strange and even bizarre to our ears. Is this because we have become so accustomed to technological fixes, or is it because the suggestion has no basis in Christian thinking?

I raise this improbable possibility because we are surrounded by calls for moratoria on medical developments, as if it is self-evident that the type of work being undertaken at present is unacceptable and unwise. By contrast, past developments were self-evidently beneficial. But this is not the case. New developments nearly always raise eyebrows, because their unusual nature is a source of consternation. Sometimes theological objections are raised, as in the case of the introduction of anaesthesia in childbirth. These reactions are not confined to science, since even many of the great composers, who now seem to be such stalwarts of tradition, were innovators in their day – introducing new instruments into orchestral pieces, using them in outlandish ways, and thinking completely outside the box.

And so, as one now looks back on these directions within

medicine, the usual response is one of gratitude. Within Christian circles there has been little interest in viewing infectious scourges as reflections of God's will, things that should be accepted as an inevitable consequence of his mysteriously ineffable purposes. They have been seen as evils to be combated and overcome. Children dying at the age of four or five has not been viewed as a blessing, but as a tragedy about which something should be done. Populations decimated by smallpox have been viewed as populations in dire need of assistance. Cholera was not viewed as anyone's friend, but as a blight on urban populations and whole societies. Similarly, today, countries plagued by malnutrition and malaria urgently need assistance, regardless of the political instability and internecine strife that so often precipitate these tragedies.

Efforts such as these have depended on the creativity and compassion of human beings. In this way human societies have been transformed, and continue to be transformed. Lifespan has been extended, infant-mortality rates have decreased dramatically, and the overall quality of people's lives and experiences have improved. The significance of this transformation becomes only too apparent when healthy communities in developed countries are compared to the misery and limited expectations of communities living at bare subsistence levels. The former are in a position to explore true human potential, whereas the latter are not. The former can develop and mature as human beings, whereas the efforts of the latter are confined to providing the most basic of needs for their continued existence.

These historical examples are all characterised by attempts to diminish suffering and remedy defects. They all have plausible therapeutic goals, which open up the possibility of bringing wholeness and purpose to real human beings contending with a broken, fragmented world. Goals such as these are not exclusively biological ones; sometimes the spiritual dimension is far more important. Nevertheless, the biological is generally not too far from the surface. It would be difficult to argue that these are anything other than goals consistent with Christian values and aspirations. The aim of improving the human condition accords well with a serious attempt to enhance human dignity and expand people's capacities to relate better to God and to one another.

From this one can derive what amounts to a general principle, namely that there is no spiritual virtue in being complacent with the alterable, because this denotes nothing more than an acceptance of sloth and mediocrity. On the other hand, it is important to learn contentment with the *un*alterable, anything that is currently beyond our ability to change for the better (MacKay, 1979). This will prevent us grasping after the unattainable and utilising technology inappropriately and excessively. Christians are in a good position to attain a balance between the two, depending as it does on a high view of human existence tempered by a realistic assessment of human mortality.

Occasionally one comes across statements that some at least of the tragedies encountered within our world are examples of God punishing the wickedness of individuals, or more often whole societies. There is a tendency to make such statements about contemporary developments, including medical technologies. However, it does not lie within the province of human beings to make judgements of this nature. Further, I am not aware of any examples of public policy, including policy with a Christian foundation, that are based on such assertions.

The world is not an unchanging given, in that we interfere in numerous ways with nature. We need to ask what changes will advance human welfare in this balanced fashion?

However understandable it is to be cautious over the directions of technology, caution has to be balanced against the immensely destructive forces of nature out of control.

Manipulation too far?

As one surveys the type of interventions I have just sketched, there is a sense in which they lie outside human beings themselves. They give the impression of being external to what we are as people. I believe this is deceptive, since they have had vast implications for the quality and character of human life. As such they constitute a good. After all, the lives of many people have been substantially improved. They can, therefore, be described as *beneficent manipulation*. They illustrate forms of manipulation that can readily be interpreted in positive terms. But might there also be maleficent manipulation?

One definition of *maleficent manipulation* is that it distorts what people are as images of God. Is it possible to identify any such distortion? One can speculate and imagine some forms of radical genetic modification, multi-organ replacements, or massive neural transplants or artificial interference in brain function. It may be that manipulation of this order could actually alter the moral status of those who have been manipulated, to reflect the whims of their human creators rather than the purposes of God. Instead of living as moral agents they would be reduced to being little more than the handmaidens of their manipulators. These are disturbing possibilities, even though they may be nothing more than idle and misleading speculation. Against this background, consider some questions.

What would be the motives of the manipulators? If these procedures were to be carried out with the intention of benefiting the person being manipulated, if they had been subjected to rigorous scientific assessment, and if fully informed consent had been provided for the procedure, there would seem to be no good reason for objecting in principle. On the other hand, if none of these strictures holds, they are unacceptable scientifically, ethically and theologically.

Would these modified individuals still be able to respond to their world, to other people and to God? Would they still be capable of understanding and of having meaningful relationships with others in the human community, of having values and hopes, of planning for the future, of demonstrating love and compassion, of making choices, and of worshipping? These capacities encompass something of what it means to be "in the image and likeness of God". Consequently, they constitute the benchmark for deciding on the validity of any procedures along these lines.

Many individuals are currently manipulated in quite radical ways. Artificial body parts are commonly used; many operations involve removing some pathology and replacing it with an un-physiological way of functioning. However, if these improve the quality of life of the patients, there appear to be no ethical or theological objections to employing them. Within a Christian perspective, the end result is to be welcomed and God is to be thanked for working through what has been made possible by the Godlike creativity and abilities of human beings, even though highly sophisticated technologies might be employed. Conversely, if individuals were to be modified to a degree at which they could no longer function in genuinely human ways, by making choices, exercising their freedom, or being aware of themselves, their status as God's agents would have been thrown into question. But if these restrictions do not follow, no matter how technologically manipulated they may be, they will continue to reflect the crucial relational features of a personal God.

Manipulating genes

This general outline may pose few problems, but as we move into the genetic realm we may have moved into substantially different territory. The concern often expressed is that, with genetic manipulation, we move into the locus of what makes us human. Genes are different; some even refer to them, or at least DNA, as sacred. The overwhelming concerns are illustrated by the following quote from an American pastor:

> We stand today at a crossroads where quite literally the future of the human race is at stake. I do not mean the *survival* of the human race, but something more sinister: the altering of the very concept of *what it means to be human*. The issue is not whether future generations shall live; the issue is what future people – if we call them such – shall be like. (Erwin W. Lutzer, 2003)

We have already encountered those writers who appear to suggest that the maintenance of genetic uncertainty in the reproductive realm is important for maintaining human dignity (Meilaender, 1998). This is because it imparts to the whole of sexual reproduction an unknown and uncontrolled aura, which some view as having Christian significance. Hence, manipulation of this realm is going against something fundamental to Christians – it is putting unwarranted control into human hands. Other Christians dislike lottery connotations in a genetic context, because they interpret this as detracting from God's interest in and control of every one of our genes. Quite apart from the speculative nature of this position, it makes God the author of every genetic disease, which one imagines is not its intention.

Coming back to the genetic lottery, one has to ask why there is virtue in mystery rather than understanding. When the genetic lottery goes seriously wrong, resulting in distressing diseases, we attempt to rectify what has gone wrong. Traditionally this is done indirectly, by manipulating the results of the genetic errors using conventional medical approaches. But is there any difference in principle between this and directly influencing genetic combinations? Both are forms of control.

Underlying all such niceties is a more fundamental query, and this is whether or not we are prepared to accept what the genetic lottery turns up (or what genetic combinations turn up, if one dislikes the lottery concept). The history of medicine and medical intervention suggests that we are not prepared to do this. Diseases galore have been tackled, even though many of them have genetic bases. Consequently, to accept whatever the genetic lottery doles out is genetic fatalism, and a rejection of the wholeness of human existence. There is no difference in principle between the genetic lottery, the accident lottery or the environmental lottery. There are chance elements in all three, and all three may have dire repercussions for the character of human life. We either tackle all three, or we ignore all three.

In principle, there is nothing sacrilegious about modifying DNA or any processes at the commencement of human life; they have the potential for extending the work of God, as long as the modification is guided by the well-being of humans (Cole-Turner, 1993). Such creativity accords with God's creative activity in nature.

This is not carte blanche for carrying every modification imaginable at the genetic level, any more than it would be at any other level. Discernment is always required, and a weighing of possibilities is always called for. This is not an argument that everyone should be born "normal", since undue emphasis on some idealised "normal" is itself a stumbling

block. Any hint of searching for some ideal in human existence is a religious rather than a scientific quest. We have no
idea what a genetic ideal would look like, and it is highly
unlikely that there is any such thing. Consequently, any suggestion that science will reveal such an ideal is deeply flawed
and seriously misguided. A Christian perspective is far more
realistic than this, with its concern for the weak and disadvantaged, the unlovely and the impoverished, the outsiders
and the downtrodden.

But could genetic knowledge go too far? Imagine the following:

> It is possible to envisage a world where the genetic make-up of
> individuals is totally known and, hence, is open to being
> analysed by others. Genetic "chips" are available, and these
> could be used to read out our individual genetic make-up.
> Theoretically, everything that could be known about us geneti-
> cally is open to scrutiny. Information is available about the
> functioning of our kidneys or brain, the chances of our mani-
> festing a whole range of cancers or heart disease, and even our
> ability to cope with stress, or our proneness to depression. This
> is where the human genome project may lead, presenting as it
> does enticing therapeutic vistas, or alternatively, dire predic-
> tions of abusive control and a loss of human freedom. Of those
> two paths, it is the negative one that is so often highlighted.

Genetic knowledge of this order could enhance people's
understanding of themselves and their world. For instance,
instead of having to think vaguely about, say, cholesterol levels, which may or may not have the significance attributed to
them for particular individuals, *I* would know whether these
levels should be taken seriously in *my* case. Others would have
the same information for themselves. Medicine would have
become personalised and far more specific than anything we

can even contemplate now. Unfortunately, this might not be the panacea some claim, since it is not known whether we could cope with such detailed information. And how many people would actually make use of it to enhance their well-being is yet another vast unknown. The medicalisation of life would be truly with us, and it might prove overbearing.

And there is yet another crucial consideration. Even in a world characterised by this level of genetic foreknowledge, there would still be an intimate connection between people's genes and the numerous environmental factors that will have influenced genetic expression since the first few days of their embryonic existence. A strong predisposition to develop stomach cancer is affected by dietary, neuroendocrine, external environmental, and attitudinal factors. And, in the last analysis, it is a person who develops stomach cancer, and not a set of genes. In other words, even in some future world of genetic foreknowledge, the crucial context will still be that of people in their wholeness, and not genes in some aseptic, depersonalised cellular compartments. A predisposition for a disease or behavioural trait is not the same as having that disease or expressing that trait.

And then, of course, human lives are blighted by accidents, traumas of various descriptions, and injuries galore. Our ideals are rudely smashed by actions having nothing whatever to do with genetic perfection or imperfection. This is where realistic assessments of the human condition and of human aspirations come into their own. Christian contributions come to the fore here, with their emphasis on equal treatment for all, living for others, and refusing to be limited by scientific perspectives in isolation from a broader world view.

Nevertheless, this discussion raises a fundamental notion, which is that we can be "known" biologically ("known" genetically). For some, this is the ultimate in genetic determinism. This is an unfortunate conclusion, because the accuracy of the predictions will depend on factors additional to, and interacting with, the genetic. Just as genes contribute to what we are as people, the persons we have become influence our genes and their expression. Consequently, genetic determinism is far less of a threat than once supposed, and reductionism should be regarded solely as a methodological tool. Similar considerations apply in the realm of the brain, as we shall now see.

Manipulating the brain

What, then, about the brain? According to neural determinism, we act in certain ways or are certain sorts of people because of the brains we possess. Taken to its logical conclusion this position states that the dimensions of some brain area (or a group of nerve cell bodies known as a "nucleus"), or the synaptic connectivity between the nerve cells within some particular region, determine some aspect of that individual's lifestyle or even beliefs. Confronted by this prospect, the temptation is to move in one of two directions: either accept that physical determinism of this order is true, or reject the notion that the brain has anything to do with our thinking or attitudes.

For me, both directions are equally unsatisfactory, since they lead either towards materialism and a rejection of human freedom, or towards a brain-mind dualism. In their different ways, neither takes neuroscience seriously and neither is able to retain a holistic view of the human person (Jones, 2004a,b). What, then, should be our point of departure?

Consider ordinary brain activity, which takes place when everything appears to be functioning normally. A fundamental working assumption of most neuroscientists is that our thinking and consciousness are embodied in the activity of our brains. What this means is that a change in someone's conscious experience or personality is accompanied by a corresponding physical change in that individual's brain (MacKay, 1987a). By the same token, any changes made to the brain, say by drugs or electrical stimulation, have corresponding effects in conscious experience or personality. The precise effects depend on the particular brain region affected.

Since it is only through our conscious experience that we learn about anything at all, primacy should be given to the data of our conscious experience (MacKay, 1987b). Therefore, although mental activity is embodied in brain activity, it is just as real as brain activity. The two need each other; they are complementary. Consequently, it is appropriate to state that "I am thinking" and "I am deciding". It would be unhelpful to state that "my brain is thinking" or "my brain is deciding", as though my brain were separated in some way from "me" as a thinking and deciding individual. There is no question that "I" need my brain, but "I" am not made redundant because of dependence on my brain. What I am as a person cannot be reduced to what my brain is, as though my body and personality are simply extensions of my brain.

It is well known that specific brain regions control particular functions and responses. By stimulating various parts of the brain, one can identify certain regions that are involved in the generation of needs and desires, the ability to think and speak, and the establishment of a total behavioural repertoire. The relationships between these are both extensive and intricate, demonstrating that the brain is far more than a series of isolated units; indeed, it is the very complexity of the brain that is essential for all we consider normal about human behaviour. Even a localised, isolated fault can result in bizarre and terrifying abnormalities of personality.

Is it possible, then, to distinguish between obvious pathology and more subtle personality disorders that are sometimes associated with social deviance? This is an important distinction, because a well-recognised pathology tells us that someone is obviously ill; they are considered to be ill by the community. On the other hand, some very subtle personality disorders are far less readily diagnosed as illness, and are certainly not accepted as such by many in the community.

It is relatively straightforward to understand the manner in which tumours, say, give rise to neurological symptoms and signs. These are cases of overt pathology, where a tumour in a particular region presses on a nerve, increases the pressure within the skull, or compresses a neighbouring brain region. The resulting symptoms and signs fall squarely into the neurological category. The person is treated as a patient, and efforts are made to remove the tumour or suppress it in an appropriate manner. The intention of treatment is to return the person to their former healthy state, resuming normal activities and having exactly the same personality as they had previously.

Life is not as straightforward in some other instances. Take the case of a violent person who has come to the attention of the police, rather than turning up at a doctor's clinic. Initially, this person is a social, rather than a medical, problem. But what is the cause of this excessive violence? What if it is not simply social, but has a biological component? There have been instances where the argument has been put that the person has no choice, because the violence is due in large part to a tumour in some part of his brain. Is this individual's criminal behaviour due to an illness? Is he ill rather than bad?

In an attempt to answer such questions, considerable attention has been devoted to a nuclear mass in the brain, known as the amygdala, and also to parts of the temporal lobes of the brain. There is considerable evidence from animals and humans to show that these brain regions are involved in the expression and control of the emotions. When something goes wrong in these regions, major changes can ensue, dramatically altering crucial features of the patient's personality, including motivation, interest in life, attitudes, and value systems. Such connections cannot be entirely dismissed in some cases. However, enormous care has to be exercised in moving from here to routinely explaining extreme violence in neural terms (Valenstein, 1973). This is usually not the case, since poverty, subcultures of violence, and domestic disputes have emerged as of greater importance (Tardoff, 1998). If a tumour is present, it should be removed, but the person concerned may not be returned to normal functioning, since the tumour alone might not have been the sole cause of the violence. Environmental and social factors might also have had significant parts to play. Hence, the relation between illness and social deviance is a complex one. We are back at the role of the environment in the final expression of our biological propensities.

Scanning the private brain

A two-way interaction between our brains and what we are as people is fundamental, since our brains are influenced by everything, from education to the relationships of ordinary life, from simple memory tasks to creative intellectual activities, from years of psychological abuse to being brought up to conform to extremely taxing expectations. While this has been an underlying assumption of neuroscientists for many years, it is now relatively easy to demonstrate the relationship between simple tasks and brain activity, using non-invasive techniques such as functional magnetic resonance imaging (fMRI), and single-photon-emission computerised tomography (Farah & Wolpe, 2004). Respectively, these track radioactively tagged chemicals around the brain, and monitor the rate of blood flow in the brain (to determine the relative activity of different brain regions).

The use of such non-invasive procedures can for instance demonstrate which brain regions are functioning when people think about certain events, or memorise various tasks. In this way, the performance of patients with neurological disorders can be compared with that of control subjects. Differences can even be detected between depressed and non-depressed individuals in their response to, for example, "sad" words.

But is the use of brain scans like these going too far? Should there be an inner sanctum within us that is beyond the probing of other people? We have already encountered this type of query with regard to genetics. Just as we place a high value on privacy in our ordinary existences, in that we frequently regard our homes as a place of retreat from our public façades, is there an inner realm that should forever remain private? If we think there should be, brain scans are beginning to intrude on that privacy.

Brain-imaging equipment is being used in experimental ways to reveal people's innermost thoughts and feelings in what has been dubbed "social neuroscience". It is becoming possible to probe violent tendencies, moral reasoning, feelings of love and trust, notions of justice, and even racial prejudice. In other words, these techniques are being used to obtain information on social and behavioural issues. Going further, it may become possible to use brain images to predict how people might behave in a given situation.

Inevitable concerns surrounding this work are that information might fall into the wrong hands and be used for a variety of questionable, and possibly illegal and unethical, purposes. What it is doing, of course, is detecting the brain regions that appear to be functioning when the person is thinking or responding in various ways. As such it does not raise any new theological issues, since the person concerned is still the one who is doing the thinking and responding. The novel element is that others can, quite literally, see the brain areas involved, and once it is known what functional patterns to look for, it becomes possible to tell the person (or others) how they are thinking and even some of the attitudes they are displaying.

This is forbidding because so often we don't want to be open and completely honest with others, or with ourselves. Honesty is a novel concept. But surely this should be less of a problem for those who take the teaching of Jesus seriously (for example Matthew 6:5–6, 7:15–27, 23:1–39). Not only this, but one of the hallmarks of God's ultimate judgement on everyone will be that nothing is private. All is revealed (Matthew 25:31–46).

The inroads of fMRI inevitably raise social and ethical concerns. New subdisciplines might appear, such as neuroeconomics and neuromarketing, all replete with possible misuse. And yet, as we have seen repeatedly throughout these chapters, new developments of this nature are simply extensions of what we already do. Consequently, they raise issues already encountered in other related fields. It's the precision and apparently intrusive nature of the procedures that alarm many people, and yet the general ethical guidelines that will be needed already exist.

Brain scans serve to describe what we are like and the priorities we have, but they have no role in determining how we came to be like this or where we will go from here. Those are our decisions. A little extra honesty would undoubtedly be good for everyone, even if its novelty would be shocking to many.

Can we cope?

No matter how one tackles the range of issues dealt with in this and earlier chapters, there is no getting away from the increasing demands being made on our moral and ethical values and value systems. I sympathise with those who think we are not capable of dealing with the challenges presented by the emerging biomedical technologies. Life would certainly be simpler if they were not there to haunt us. However, we are surrounded by technologies with dramatic repercussions for our value systems. Changing social mores that do not depend at all on technological innovations challenge us just as powerfully.

My response to these challenges is not to say that we must do all we can to prevent them being adopted by society. A global decision along those lines is an admittance that our value systems, including those of Christians, cannot cope. Decisions over individual technologies need to be made on a case-by-case basis, and even when allowed within a society, whether individuals use them is yet another critical decision. Discernment and integrity are required at both levels, and this is where mature Christian reflection should come into its own, reflection that refuses to separate the technology from what we are as people.

This, in turn, presents us with the need to distinguish between the use of technologies to repair people and to manipulate them. Both are possibilities, both can eventuate, the one for the benefit of the people concerned and the other for the benefit of those carrying out the manipulation. The choices, however, are frequently not nearly as clear-cut as this contrast might suggest. We might wish otherwise, but the real world in all its grandeur and all its fallenness demands far more of us as humans made in God's image and likeness.

Chapter 8

Being Human in a Scientific World

No matter how one looks at the issues raised in the preceding chapters, one is left with a feeling of unease. My stance has largely been one of acceptance of many of the possibilities opened up by current biomedical procedures. And yet my acceptance of these possibilities has been tinged with concern. It is only too obvious to us today that the greatest of possibilities can be grotesquely abused and directed towards tragic ends. Consequently, the successes of science over the past 50 years have been compromised successes. The optimism of mid-20th century science has been replaced by pessimism, and sometimes even by antagonism towards the scientific endeavour itself. Such antagonism is as likely to be found within Christian communities as within any others.

The antagonism stems from what is viewed as the almost limitless power of science, with its ability to transform and change so many of the things we hold dear. Science by itself does not of course constitute the only source of change, and yet the extent and speed of change and its consequent ability to threaten our very essence owes much to scientific developments. Linked with this is what is regarded as the arrogance of scientists, who in the public imagination appear to hold nothing dear. All that is beautiful is fair game for being trodden underfoot by the onward march of scientific inquisitiveness and invention. Nothing is sacrosanct, not even human life.

It is no wonder that an account like this readily assumes religious overtones and even religious language. While this use of religious language is not confined to those with explicit religious convictions, it gains its power from the manner in which it appears to echo the certainties and greater social stability of the past. No matter how unreliable some of the memories and depictions may be, they exercise a powerful influence on current debate. The message to emerge is that the threat posed by science is palpable, with considerable repercussions for each of the debates touched on in the previous chapters.

For some Christians, fears of this nature are accentuated by the way in which the increasing influence of scientific developments gives the appearance of directly displacing the activity and even the role of God in the universe. We play God when we reorder what is found in nature; we design babies when we change embryos. In these ways we become creators, and take upon ourselves the mantle of God. Humans never used to act in these ways; they used to be subservient to God. But if this it true, and if science can provide us with a comfortable life, why bother with God? If the activity and explanations of science provide us with all we want, there is no longer any room for God. In this way of thinking, God and science occupy positions at opposite ends of a spectrum, and are antithetical to each another. Some Christians think like this, as do some atheists, the former opposing anything scientific and the latter anything religious or Christian.

My position has been that we would not be better off without the scientific contributions we have been considering, in spite of the fact that they have been, and will continue to be, accompanied by a range of enormous challenges. My aim in this book has been to work through major issues, especially those in the reproductive technologies, commenting on them from a Christian perspective. I believe it is possible to do this without watering down either the scientific or the Christian sides. Indeed, I would argue that the Christian viewpoint provides a workable framework within which one can gain a deeper appreciation of the comparative value of scientific developments. The two are inextricably intertwined, and it is at this interface between the developments and the challenges they raise that we perceive most clearly the dimensions of the ethical and theological questions.

The place of science in applied Christian thinking

As we have just seen, science is sometimes viewed as a threat to Christian conceptions by bringing into stark relief the relative power of science alongside the perceived power traditionally ascribed to God. If one increases, the other by definition must decrease; there is an inverse relationship between the two. I have argued against this on the grounds that, in part, God's power is demonstrated by the abilities of humans as shown through a variety of endeavours, including scientific ones. Human and divine power are not mutually exclusive opposites (see Chapter 1). While a bold statement like this hardly solves all problems in this area, it helps to place the two sets of power, and the two sets of control that go with them, in their respective positions.

However, there is an additional source of concern for some Christians, and this is the threat that science and some aspects of scientific interpretation pose for biblical interpretation. This is a more specific concern than the previous one, because it touches on an important source (some would say the only source) of Christian thinking. There can be no doubt that, for most Christian communities, the Bible is an indispensable touchstone for formulating a Christian perspective,

Christian thinking and Christian attitudes. But how far does this extend, and what are its dimensions? For instance, if it is contended that the Bible teaches that the world was created in six days 6,000 years ago, a viewpoint that bears no relationship to the scientific thought of the last 150–200 years, with its vast timescale and evolutionary framework, then these two views cannot exist alongside each other. This is an extreme example, and yet one that continues to be a source of enormous tension within conservative Christian circles. Since the existence of this alleged biblical viewpoint sits very uneasily alongside any serious scientific world view, it places certain Christian groups at the periphery of most contemporary thinking (including much Christian thinking). While this in itself does not invalidate any particular position on creation, it automatically tars them with an anti-scientific hue.

More relevant for this book are views on the beginning of human life. If the starting point of meaningful human life is placed at conception, the scientific and ethical consequences that follow are legion. But what if conception is chosen on theological grounds, since biblical interpretation is thought to warrant this? The stakes have increased very considerably, because the way is now open to head-on conflict between science and theology. Moreover, if this position is vigorously defended and promulgated by Christian groups as the only tenable position for society (let alone the church), it becomes a benchmark statement. No wonder many outside the churches consider this to be "the" religious position, the position that all Christians hold. A viewpoint that, in my view, is not central to the Christian faith has come to enshrine what is Christian in the eyes of many outside the churches. This immediately poses a problem for someone like myself, who argues along Christian lines, and hence is looked upon as being "religious", and yet rejects this stance.

These considerations by themselves are insufficient to justify the conclusion that conception (fertilisation) is an untenable starting point for human personhood. However, neither an ethical nor a theological position on a question with scientific components can ignore legitimate scientific considerations. Once this happens, the position in question loses its moorings and is cast adrift on a sea of subjectivity, making claims that allegedly have scientific backing but which in reality may have no such backing. This is illustrated by the difficulties that arise when any traditional position has built-in scientific information that is now outdated. In these circumstances, proponents may find it difficult to acknowledge that this is the case, since the scientific information has become far too closely entwined with theological or moral stances. In a sense it has become part of revealed truth, thereby assuming an authority foreign to its nature. And, by definition, any alternative scientific interpretation stands in opposition to the one scientific view that has been given the mantle of representing the traditional and "correct" position.

In my view this is what has occurred with respect to the role of conception in many church traditions, ranging from Roman Catholicism to evangelical Protestant constituencies. For different reasons, conception has become enshrined as the only legitimate depiction of the commencement of meaningful human life, carrying with it a medley of powerful theological overtones. For instance, from this point onwards embryos are to be viewed as images of God and as the objects of God's love. What is interesting is that the assurance with which conception has assumed such a decisive theological and ethical role is based on a paucity of biblical data, interpreted in a highly selective manner and bolstered by questionable scientific data, namely the genetic uniqueness of each new embryo. If this viewpoint is to retain any relationship with science and hence be of value in discussing scientific issues, its proponents have to be willing to open it up to reassessment and reinterpretation in the light of changing scientific thinking.

It is dangerous to make use of scientific data and ideas that appear to serve a particular cause, while ignoring those that do not. In these terms, the genetic uniqueness of each new embryo is a relevant piece of evidence in assessing the significance of early embryos, but by itself it is insufficient to bolster the theological claims for personal uniqueness and standing before God (see Chapters 3 and 4). Additionally, the data themselves are open to adaptation and extension. This prompts the question of where the scientific data come into the picture: are they primary pieces of evidence (possibly alongside biblical evidence) or are they secondary and confirmatory (being used to bolster positions arrived at on other grounds)? This question has been looked at in a different context in Chapter 4.

The way in which we answer this question will throw considerable light on how we tackle the issues addressed in this book. I have argued that, to the extent that a scientific perspective is relevant, it has to be allowed to make a significant contribution, albeit not an isolated one, since science alone is insufficient to answer questions of meaning and ethics. Hence, the viewpoint that conception marks the start of meaningful human life can be taken seriously only if it is supported by rigorous scientific analysis. It is not justified on the basis of the very general biblical data that are available. Similar strictures apply to any other developmental point that might be chosen as having either ethical or theological significance.

The creative nature of scientific investigations

Embedded within the previous discussion is one particular feature of scientific analysis that is relevant to considerations of the status of the human embryo. This is the way in which it always tends to push boundaries, as is its nature and ethos. If one does not accept this one will never come to terms with what science has to offer. In this sense Christian thinking will never control it, any more than it controls Christian thinking.

Scientific investigations will always be on the edge seeking out new ways of doing things and of solving problems. They are not readily constrained and they should not be so. They will, therefore, always be treading on the toes of those who have vested interests, including on some occasions vested Christian ones.

Take the example of homosexuality. For some, there is considerable danger in admitting that there might be a biological aspect to homosexuality, in the sense that the brains of at least some of those with homosexual tendencies or behaviour might have features not found in the brains of those with heterosexual leanings. If taken to extremes, efforts will be made to downplay or even censor discussion of these particular findings. However, as discussed in Chapters 5 and 7, there is ample room for such discussions, since neuroscientific findings have to be assessed and interpreted. Nevertheless, the findings by themselves do not lead to any definitive conclusions, because scientific analysis has to be seen in the light of social and theological factors. There are also scientific unknowns. Were the findings present from birth? Do they precede or follow the expression of homosexual tendencies? Do all those with such tendencies have the same neural characteristics?

In other words, the claim that certain regions of the brains of homosexuals might sometimes differ from the brains of others in society does not actually tell us very much. These findings might take on far greater explanatory powers when viewed together with other data, but in the meantime they need to be treated cautiously. This is quite different from dismissing them altogether, on the grounds that they do not fit neatly into our previous conception of what they might imply. Healthy debate requires openness to data and information, no matter what their source. Both theological interpretation and scientific insights have contributions to make to a complex area like that of homosexuality.

One particular scientific interpretation may or may not ultimately be shown to be correct. The important point is that scientific claims should be neither feared nor dismissed, but should be analysed on their merits. This does not make them right or even more appropriate than other approaches. But they should be taken into account.

The pushing of boundaries by scientific developments also has implications for the nature of bioethics, since it may give the impression that ethical reflection can do nothing other than follow scientific advance. A problem for both bioethics and theology is that the precise directions in which science moves, and therefore the questions it poses for society, are exceedingly hard – if not impossible – to predict. For instance, where will the science of stem cells and research cloning be in 2025? Is it possible to map this out in 2005, and hence establish ethical and theological guidelines for these future developments? I have my doubts, since what come first are the developments, rather than guidelines formulated by ethicists or theologians. Indeed, it is the developments themselves that serve to stimulate the formulation of guidelines, which in their turn provide assistance for further exploration. This may be regarded as an unsatisfactory, and even a potentially dangerous, situation, and yet it is difficult to see any alternative. The most that ethicists or theologians can do, in the absence of knowing what precise scientific movements will occur, is to propose general directions that may or may not be appropriate or even helpful.

Calls for the imposition of moratoria "while the ethics are sorted out" tend to be too diffuse to be useful. What might this mean in practice? Take an example. PGD, as we have seen, can be used to determine the sex of early embryos (see Chapters 1 and 2). But how does one determine the rightness or other-wise of determining the sex of an embryo as a prelude to implanting embryos of one sex rather than the other? Under what circumstances, if any, might this be allowable? These debates have been around for years, and yet it is only a tech-nique like PGD that imparts urgency to them. It also imparts a feel of reality, since the range of conditions where sex selec-tion might be relevant is dependent upon the techniques available.

Similar comments apply to theological considerations. In the absence of long-standing, generally accepted and specific biblical or theological teaching on this matter, theological vis-tas have been very general ones. It is only the availability of PGD that has transformed the debate from the nebulous to the specific. But, once again, it is the science that has come first.

Ethics and theology have the important task of reflecting on the directions and aspirations of science. This is more piv-otal than is generally realised, since it provides the ethos within which the science is undertaken. However, this can be effectively carried out only if there is ongoing interaction between these disciplines and specific science projects. This is not a theoretical task to be undertaken from an armchair; it requires insight into the science in question: its methodology, its pitfalls and its potential.

Only in this way can we move away from the idea that scientists are autonomous beings, experimenting in whatever way suits them. Scientists, like everyone else within a community, function according to the aspirations of that community. While they may be in the privileged (and even powerful) position of determining the exact form their studies are to take, they too are moral beings functioning within the general ethos of their society. For instance, a society that does not tolerate the purchase of body organs such as kidneys from the disadvantaged will, by its very nature, discourage even the most foolhardy transplant surgeons from undertaking this highly questionable procedure. By contrast, a society with few scruples in this regard will find that a few surgeons may well go in this direction. While this in no way exonerates the surgeons, what they are or are not prepared to do is related to the character of the society in which they are functioning as professionals.

All this might be fine in affluent societies, but what about the two-thirds world, where even the most basic medical care is lacking? Surely, some argue, sophisticated reproductive science is a blot on the moral landscape as long as this appalling inequality continues. Rectify this as a first priority before indulging in the fripperies of expensive and unnecessary ways around infertility for the rich. All arguments along these lines contain within them a strong grain of uncomfortable truth. This inequality has to be faced up to, because it represents an indictment of global health care that allows or even encourages the self-serving practices of many well-off countries. Nevertheless, is it a relevant argument to be used against creative attempts to overcome infertility and discover more about basic embryological processes?

The trouble with this argument is that it is being used selectively against one endeavour – reproductive science. If applied consistently, it would have repercussions for every area of our lives: from housing to education, from health care to welfare, from roading to communication networks. There is inequality in every area of life, and, iniquitous as much of this is, no useful purpose is served by constraining scientific initiative in one area simply because this particular area has theological and ethical overtones that disturb some sections of the community. Our concerns should be to put pressure on the political system to ensure that the benefits that might emanate from this work will, in the long term, have beneficial effects worldwide. This is not impossible, even though its implementation lies well beyond the scope of the scientific community.

God's care versus human care

In Chapter 1 we encountered an apparent contrast between human and divine control, with its potential to generate conflict. The reason for this is that, as human control has become increasingly precise, the questions it raises have also become increasingly precise. This precision forces us to consider whether we expect God's control to be expressed in comparably precise terms. This, in turn, elicits a theological query, namely whether God micro-manages our lives.

Biblical justification for the latter appears to be found in the words of Jesus when he made the comment that "even the hairs of your head are all counted" (Luke 12:7). Is this to be taken literally, and is the modern equivalent the counting of every skin cell, mucosal cell, nerve cell and gene? The context within which Jesus made this comment was that of reassuring his followers that God would protect them from those who set out to destroy them and their faith, thereby separating them from Christ and the new way of life to be found in him. To make his point he drew a contrast between the value of human beings and that of sparrows. Since God's concern extends to sparrows, surely it will also encompass his followers who are of far greater value (Luke 12:4–7). Therefore, they were not to be afraid when confronted by those who wished to destroy them. God knew them, even down to the level of the hairs on their head. Later in the same dialogue, Jesus told them not to worry about what they would eat or wear. Since God's care extends to birds such as ravens and flowers such as lilies, in spite of their brief and fragile existences, his care for his disciples should be unquestioned. To emphasise this, he reminded them of the obvious fact that worrying would not enable them to add to their height or extend their lives (Luke 12:22–31).

What we have in this discourse is a view of God's *care*, not his control. Except in some illnesses it doesn't really matter how many hairs we have. And even then it is not generally the most important issue in life. What would be the value of God's controlling every single hair on our head (or body)? It is far more important to know that he cares for us, as evidenced by his concern for even the detailed aspects of our lives, including our genes, cells, organs and body systems. What matters is not the exact number of hairs we have or even the precise formulation of our genes (important as the latter are), but the manner in which we are able to cope with the hairs and genes we do or do not have. And our coping is against a background of God's care and concern for us as people.

It is for this reason that the heading of this section refers to care rather than control: "God's care versus human care". As the range of human abilities is extended by scientific achievements, the pressing issue is the way in which humans utilise these abilities. Human control over biological and other processes is increasing, but it will never be complete. Nevertheless, regardless of how extensive or otherwise this is, the challenge is to direct these abilities in ways that will help individuals and communities. Do we care enough for others to direct our newly found expertise to help those in greatest need? If debate centred more on care than control, it would demonstrate the centrality of a God-orientated perspective rather than push this perspective to the periphery.

The role of suffering in infertility

Debates on means of circumventing infertility frequently include assertions that the suffering of the infertile is of a different order from the suffering of those with cancer or dementia. The underlying message is that infertility is not a disease, with the result that those who are infertile are not suffering. This leads to expressions of concern at the extent of the technological efforts sometimes employed to bypass infertility and have a child, whereas the use of high technology procedures to alleviate (other) diseases is accepted. This takes on theological dimensions when the former is seen as antipathetic to God's way of doing things, whereas the latter is in accordance with it.

The concern is magnified when the desire to bring new beings into the world by technological means is viewed alongside the number of nascent beings destroyed by abortion, as well as the children, albeit limited in number, who are available for adoption. Surely, it is argued, there can be no grounds for using expensive technology to overcome obstacles to childbearing when so much developing human life is being wasted. Even worse, the planet is overpopulated, and the utilisation of expensive resources to increase the population in some countries when there are high rates of infant mortality and malnutrition in others is untenable. This is a multifaceted argument that does have some legitimacy, and in an ideal world the contrasts would not be nearly as great. However, it overlooks numerous other considerations.

The inconsistency between societies is deplorable, and far more convincing efforts to contain it are called for than those currently being undertaken. However, this is a global problem, not an individual one. Why penalise individuals longing for a child on the ground of social inequities? This is not done in any other areas, such as living conditions, health care or education. Neither are the fertile prevented from bringing children into the world, even though this could be worsening the population situation. The evil of excessively liberal abortion policies is not the responsibility of the infertile, who should not be punished on account of them. Society may indeed be ethically inconsistent, but this is society's problem, not that of the infertile.

In the light of these considerations, I argue that infertile couples should be assessed on their merits. Whatever the precise nature of their suffering, and regardless of how it compares with that of the cancer sufferer, it is suffering that needs to be taken seriously. The effects of the suffering will vary enormously between couples (and particularly between affected women). Each case requires individual assessment; otherwise we could be castigated for failing to respond to the cries of the needy. It is not for outsiders to judge the severity or otherwise of the infertility, or the measures to be taken to attempt to alleviate it. That is the realm of professional judgement and discernment.

But what is suffering? It is remarkably easy to see it exclusively in terms of the suffering of illness and disease. While this is a component, it is peripheral when approached from a biblical perspective. It is true that Jesus healed (see, for example, Mark 3:1-12, 5:21-43, 8:22-26, 9:14-29; Luke 7:1-17), demonstrating that he had pity on those who were ill, since healing was part of his ministry of making people whole. However, he did not heal everyone who could have been healed, and he also placed it within the perspective of his coming to reveal the kingdom of God. Hence, it had explicit spiritual overtones, manifesting as it did the power of God and the character of the ministry of Jesus.

Reference to 1 Peter 4:12–19 in the New Testament shows that the suffering Peter was dealing with was largely the suffering of persecution. From this passage it emerges that these early Christians suffered because they were Christians, on some occasions as a consequence of their wrongdoing, and also because they were ordinary human beings – just like everyone else. How, though, were they to suffer? Did being Christians make any difference?

Peter argues that suffering is *normal* and is to be expected. It is referred to here as a fiery ordeal. It's a trial that is to have a positive outcome. Peter in no way underestimates the difficulties faced by these Christians, but he wants them to see God's good purpose behind the difficulties. They are to use these difficulties to grow stronger in their faith, and through them to glorify God. In a sense, therefore, they are to learn to *rejoice in suffering*, especially when the suffering comes from being faithful to Christ. This, he contends, is a means of actually sharing in Christ's sufferings, and of making Christians more like Christ.

We can say, then, that suffering of some description is essential, since the way in which we respond to suffering is one of the means by which the quality of our lives may improve. From a Christian perspective, God is glorified through faithfulness in the midst of discouragements and possibly even overt opposition. God's hand is to be recognised during testing and uncomfortable times, and in coping with situations we would much rather avoid.

How do these points help us think about the suffering encountered in illness and infertility? This form of suffering is common to humanity, and is to be tackled by all available means at our disposal. However, these means might let us down and the suffering might not be assuaged, whether the lesion is in the liver or the reproductive system. While technological approaches are to be used as appropriate, the ultimate context within which the suffering is to be tackled is via an acknowledgement that God first suffered in Christ and continues to be affected by the suffering of humanity. Unlikely as it might sound, God has purposes for his people through suffering. This applies equally to the suffering of disease and infertility. There is no reason to distinguish between the two, whether or not we consider infertility to be a disease. Some infertile people suffer very considerably, and it is this that is the crux of the issue; not all will end up with a baby, regardless of the procedures employed. But neither will all be cured whatever the disease.

Since we live in a world embedded in suffering, it would be foolhardy to expect medical science to eliminate it. Such an agenda would prove deeply misleading. In addition, as the passage from Peter's letter makes clear, there are positive aspects to suffering; we can learn a great deal from it, we come to realise that even God suffers, and that what is significant is our response to it. This is not an argument for seeking out suffering, or for doing nothing to avoid it or to mitigate its effects. The suffering of disease or infertility is part of a far larger picture, with theological as well as clinical aspects. A balance is essential between striving endlessly for good health or perfect babies, and moving gradually in these general directions at the individual and societal levels, realising that the goals that will be achieved will frequently be limited ones. Under no circumstances is the agenda to be set by unachievable idealistic goals.

Is enhancement to be feared?

Running throughout the topics in this book has been the interplay between normality and abnormality, therapy and enhancement. In Chapter 2 I drew a contrast between the healthy (H) and super-healthy (SH), the latter being those who had been specifically enhanced in some way. However, even there I had concerns about this distinction, on the grounds that those who had been enhanced would only have been "improved" in one or two quite specific respects. In practice they might be H+ rather than SH. This illustrates a difficulty repeatedly encountered when discussing therapy and enhancement, and this is whether the boundaries between the two are nearly as well defined as generally thought.

When I walk into many pharmacies and large stores, the first phenomena I usually encounter are the cosmetics counters, which to me are superb examples of enhancement emporia. The assistants are usually glowing examples of enhanced humans, at least as far as their faces and hands are concerned. There might be nothing whatsoever wrong with this phenomenon, but for me it raises the question of what is normal and what is enhanced. Is facial make-up intended to restore individuals to their normal appearance, or to make them appear better than they could ever look under routine circumstances?

Similar, if more poignant, questions can also be asked of plastic surgery. There are some cases where it has the very clear task of restoring someone's appearance (following severe burns or other injuries) to some semblance of normality. In yet others, its aim is to provide an individual born with major deformities with something far more akin to what is generally considered to fall within the range of the anatomically normal. There is no question that these intrusions are therapeutic, and in no sense could they be seen as transgressing the boundaries of normality. But there are others, which are far less clear. The individuals undergoing the plastic surgery are not ill by any normal criteria, although they might see themselves as being substandard or as having certain unfortunate bodily characteristics. They could live perfectly well without the surgery, and they have no problem in holding down positions in society. They relate well with their family and friends, even if they think they could relate better. These examples of cosmetic surgery would appear to fall into the enhancement category, and yet even here we begin to get the feeling that in some instances at least the borderline is less clear than we might like.

The trouble is that there will always be borderline cases, where the criteria are not clear-cut. Not only this, the criteria change with time. What was acceptable in 1950 might not have been acceptable in 2000, let alone in 2050. The expectations of normality change, a feature encountered in every area of life and not just in medicine. The comforts taken for granted in so many societies in the early years of the 21st century were luxuries enjoyed by few 50 years ago; so with medicine. Our expectations of what constitute good health and normal life expectancy today have changed out of all recognition since the early years of the 20th century. Moreover, our expectations bear no resemblance to those of many people today living in the two-thirds world. Which is normal? Or has normality changed? I'd suggest it is the latter. The dimensions of normality are never static, and it is this that poses such great problems for us.

In view of this, we return to the indistinct borderlands between therapy and enhancement. There is a continuum between the two, the dimensions of which keep on changing. Moreover, when thinking about normality one has to define what it encompasses at any particular time in any particular situation. Consequently, it is foolhardy to construct theological expectations based on the shifting sands of fashion and capability. Nevertheless, this still leaves a chasm of expectation and anticipation between the extremes of normality and enhancement.

No matter how unclear the issues in some instances, the thrust of decision-making is to lie in an assessment of the good or ill that might emanate from whatever alterations are undertaken. Any fears we have should spring from our own intentions and actions, our desire to improve life or use it for arrogant and overweening purposes, to enhance life as God intended or detract from it. This is not a fear of technology per se or of medical treatments per se, but of what we ourselves are and of how we do or do not employ our skills in the service of others.

Nevertheless, some are not convinced. Pellegrino (2004) has concerns that span the whole of the medical enterprise. He defines enhancement as an intervention that goes beyond the goals of medicine as they have traditionally been viewed, and he sees this as part of the medicalisation of every facet of human existence. Pellegrino wishes to avoid making physicians into enhancement therapists and to avoid transforming therapy into what he describes as a "happiness nostrum", rather than a true healing enterprise. The framework for these concerns is that enhancement provides hopes for an earthly paradise for those who no longer believe in an afterlife. In no way do I disagree with the essence of these concerns, if enhancement inevitably implies distortions that reinterpret the therapeutic in radical new ways. The nub of the debate is to determine what constitutes a distortion.

Similar comments apply to Sandel's (2004) case against perfection. His concern is with what he views as the drift to mastery with its associated ethic of wilfulness, leading to "hyperparenting" built on the hubris of designing parents who seek to master the mystery of birth. His desire is that we retain an ethic of giftedness, according to which we appreciate children as gifts, and reject enhancement that seeks perfection. For Sandel, we must reject wilfulness, dominion and moulding, in favour of giftedness, reverence and beholding. Once again, I have considerable sympathies with these concerns, but I do not see them as inevitable concomitants of the intrusion of technology into the reproductive process. I am with Sandel in wishing to see ourselves as creatures of God, accepting that we are not wholly responsible for the way we are, but I do not believe this leads to an automatic rejection of all forms of technological improvement.

A final look at embryos

Conflict and sacrifice

Since the status of the embryo and the relevance of this for the ESC debate have been dealt with at some length in Chapters 3 and 4, it might seem superfluous to raise again the question of how we determine what may or may not be done to human embryos. I am doing so because I consider that the discussion should incorporate reference to the exigencies of being human.

Discussions of the possibility that human embryos might be sacrificed as part of IVF procedures or in research are generally undertaken in isolation from other instances where human life may be sacrificed. This allows commentators to view human embryos in protectionist terms, ring-fencing them in ways that are not possible for post-natal human beings. It is in this context that the loss of human life in war is sometimes raised as an analogy that might profitably be employed when discussing the circumstances under which embryonic life might be sacrificed. However, this analogy tends to be dismissed as irrelevant and unjustified.

The analogy with war aims at making the point that the killing of human beings is justified under certain circumstances. In war there is no question regarding the status of these people; they are human persons, made in the image of God. Not only this but the range of people killed is wide: combatants, civilians, adults, children, fetuses and embryos. Many of these are essentially innocent, in the sense that they are not protagonists, and may even be too young to have any views of the rightness or otherwise of the policies of those in power in their countries. They are killed because they get caught up in a conflict over which they have no control. Their deaths might be justified as collateral in a conflict between good and evil, where the interests of one society or way of life are being defended against the threat posed by an alternative (and by definition inferior) way of life. Once war is legitimised, the deaths of people, including innocent people, become inevitable.

These comments apply regardless of the nature of the conflicts, or the reasons for them. Some goods are being placed above the value of human life. Once war is justified, the destruction of human life becomes inevitable, even if every effort is made to minimise the loss of life and to restrict it to combatants. In other words, human life is sacrificed in wars, the main consideration being whether the wars can be justified.

In view of this, it has to be asked whether the same considerations cannot be applied to human embryos in the laboratory. Ethical and theological discussions generally compare these embryos to adult patients. Since embryos cannot consent to procedures undertaken on them (supremely their own destruction), these procedures should not be carried out. Similarly, since it is unethical to kill adults, it is unethical to kill embryos. However, these analogies are exceedingly restrictive, the underlying assumption being that embryos are equivalent to fully-fledged human persons. They also ignore situations in which adults and children are justifiably killed. Let us then turn to the war analogy, which has been explored by Gilbert Meilaender (2001) in the context of the possible use of ESCs.

Meilaender (2001) argues that two moral judgements are involved in meeting the criteria for the sacrifice of life in war (an argument based on ideas elaborated by Walzer, 1977). When is it permissible to go to war – the theory of aggression. What is it permissible to do in war – the war convention. If these two questions can be answered satisfactorily, the war may be described as just. However, things are not always this clear, resulting on some occasions in *dilemmas of war*. Extreme circumstances may arise, when the rules of war may be ignored to ensure victory and avoid a greater injustice. In these circumstances, there is an enemy who must be defeated, since victory by the enemy will threaten everything decent in our lives. In these situations of supreme emergency, it becomes strategically and morally necessary to override the war convention: everything possible should be done to win the war.

When we turn to the use of ESCs, does the threat posed by serious diseases and intense suffering present circumstances that represent such a supreme emergency? If this is the case, and if research utilising ESCs has a high chance of leading to major advances in understanding and treatment, it may be legitimate to conduct this type of research regardless of one's view of the status of the embryo. This is because the war con-vention, with its usual built-in strictures, can be ignored (for a fuller discussion of the arguments in this section and the following one, see Towns, 2004).

Take Alzheimer's disease as an example. This war is against an undefeated foe that wreaks immeasurable pain and suffering on its enemies, and currently defeat is imminent and death inevitable. Since five million people suffer from dementia in the United States alone, this disease represents an enemy of considerable magnitude. This example satisfies the criterion of *moral necessity* for supreme emergency, since it is an enemy that must be defeated (Towns, 2004). And because ESCs represent a tool that could potentially alleviate suffering and improve the quality of life for sufferers of AD, their use can be justified.

What, then, about *strategic necessity*? Is there any alternative to the use of ESCs, using either traditional approaches or ASCs? The pros and cons of ESCs and ASCs have already been outlined (see Chapter 4), from which it can be argued that the lack of treatment options for many diseases, in particular for neurodegenerative diseases, and the potential of ESCs to supply treatment options, provide grounds for strategic necessity (Towns, 2004).

In view of these considerations there are grounds for justifying the use of ESCs, even if the embryo is given a high status. There are compelling reasons why embryos should be sacrificed for a higher good, that of improving the health of people in the community, an improvement that can be brought about only through research on the earliest stages of embryonic existence. Of course this analysis can be challenged, by arguing that ESCs are not as central as I have indicated. However, that is a scientific argument, and has to be carried out on that basis. The approach I have taken can also be criticised because I have accepted that the conventions of war can, on occasion, be overridden. But, given these provisos, the war analogy provides a surprising entrée into ESC research without challenging views on the status of the embryo.

This discussion highlights the need for ethical consistency. For example, if the sacrifice of human life is justified in war because of the interests of the common good, it may be difficult to argue against a loss of embryonic life that equally benefits the common good. This argument is perhaps more compelling when it is borne in mind that embryos are not capable of sentience or suffering, unlike other humans who under certain circumstances might be sacrificed. Even more problematic is an argument against the sacrifice of human embryos in research when embryos are sacrificed routinely as part of IVF procedures. In other words, it is inconsistent to argue against the sacrifice of human life in embryo research in societies where IVF is performed.

Innocence

It is commonly contended that human embryos should be provided with greater protection than other humans, on account of their vulnerability and innocence. Meyer (2000) argues that it is only those individuals who commit no grave injustices against others who retain a right to life in the strictest sense. This is because, in his opinion, a defining circumstance of the right-to-life is innocence. The embryo is always innocent of wrongdoing and, therefore, should be protected regardless of the perceived benefits to society that might result from its destruction.

In this view, human embryos are innocent because they have not harmed or attempted to harm another life, or, indeed, their own. By definition, embryos have not done anything wrong, but, by implication, neither have they done anything "right". Embryos have not benefited anyone else, in the same way that they have not harmed anyone. This point is of importance when attempting to balance the value of the embryo against the value of those lives that might be bettered by the advent of stem-cell therapies (Towns, 2004).

There are two opposing terms here, wrongdoing and "rightdoing". To unpack this contrast, consider the balance between the value of an "innocent" embryo and the value of an elderly woman suffering from AD. The embryo might have done nothing wrong and, therefore, be innocent when compared to the woman, who would have done wrong in her lifetime. However, she would also have done "right" in that she would have contributed to the benefit of others and society.

It can be argued that an embryo gives joy to the pregnant mother and/or couple who delight in the pregnancy and the thought of giving birth to a child. However, an argument such as this is of little relevance to the specific sources of ESCs, which will have been donated by an IVF clinic or created in the laboratory specifically for research.

A choice has to be made between a potential life that has done neither right nor wrong, and a fully developed person who has contributed both good and bad, right and wrong. Innocence cannot be viewed in isolation from the interests of potential recipients of stem-cell therapies. By itself, innocence fails to provide a convincing basis for preserving the life of an embryo (Towns, 2004).

A second complication is that ESCs may contribute to therapies of benefit to young adults, children and fetuses, all of whom can be seen as manifesting varying degrees of innocence. What this means is that stem cells derived from "innocent" embryos could be used to combat the disease, alleviate the suffering and save the lives of other "innocent" beings, that is, children and fetuses. With fetuses, the source of the stem cells and the likely recipient are equally innocent.

Moreover, if ESCs are derived from surplus embryos resulting from IVF, and are subsequently used in *in utero* therapies, the notion of innocence could be used to argue in favour of research rather than against it. This is because surplus IVF embryos will be destroyed, regardless of whether or not they are used for ESC research or therapies. The notion of innocence argues in favour of the use of these cells in providing cures for diseases and disorders that will cause death *in utero*.

Consequently, the notion of innocence is inadequate justification for protecting the embryo, since it fails to weigh wrongdoing against rightdoing. It also fails to address the manner in which stem cells may save the lives of many other "innocent" embryos and fetuses. In other words, the notion of innocence should not be viewed as an isolated value, but in relation to other lives we wish to save and benefit.

Can the embryonic impasse be bypassed?
As we have seen on a number of occasions, a sticking point in the debate on ESCs is that an embryo (blastocyst) with the potential to become a future individual is destroyed. While only some refer to this as the killing or even murder of embryos, theological and ethical issues might disappear if ESCs could be obtained without the existence, albeit transitory, of a blastocyst. It is highly likely that this will be accomplished at some future time, and when it occurs the debate on ESCs will dramatically change. At present this is no more than a theoretical possibility, and so may not justify even cursory discussion, but a member of President Bush's Council on Bioethics has raised it as a way around some of the theological and ethical issues (Cook, 2004).

A procedure termed *altered nuclear transfer* has been postulated as a means of engineering a human egg to generate cells with the full potential of ESCs but without forming an actual embryo. In this procedure, DNA from a donor's cell (for example a skin cell) would be implanted into a human egg that had had its nucleus removed. On dividing, it is speculated that the egg would produce embryonic-type stem cells. By turning off a gene responsible for the formation of the trophectoderm, the latter would not form and the cells would eventually die. Hence, there would be no viable blastocyst.

This idea, which might or might not work in practice, is regarded as a way round the destruction of human embryos. In other words, one can be resolutely opposed to obtaining stem cells from embryos, but in favour of obtaining them (or something very much like them) in this way. But is this mass of cells an embryo, and what is the difference between an entity like this that is prevented from developing into a blastocyst, and a blastocyst that is prevented from developing further by silencing the gene needed to form the nervous system?

No matter what conclusion one comes to, the degree of manipulation being undertaken is considerable. On behalf of those who complain that scientists are playing God in other contexts, one has to ask how these manipulations escape that opprobrium. But isn't this getting very close to a matter of semantics?

If an embryo is defined as a group of cells capable of developing into an ongoing individual (regardless of the species), both fertilised and cloned blastocysts are, in principle, embryos. But if further development is not possible, because of inbuilt or external limitations, they are not embryos according to this definition. What then becomes of the importance so often ascribed to fertilisation (or conception)?

Ultimately, what is occurring according to this proposal is manipulation of human tissue with the intention of obtaining stem cells capable of developing into cell and tissue lines. Clearly, these are not derived from adult tissue, but they are derived from a manipulated egg. If this is of no ethical or theological consequence, one has to question whether obtaining ESCs from blastocysts incapable of developing further because of their environment is a substantially different process.

Being human

What a pity human life isn't so much simpler and more straightforward than it actually is. What a pity so much has to be so subjective. Wouldn't it be wonderful if we could stand back and compare various possibilities in neat objective terms, marking everything out of ten, approving of those procedures that scored five or more, and rejecting those that scored less than five? Objectivity would reign supreme, and both theology and ethics would become truly scientific! All murky territory would disappear, and life would be simple. Since procedure A scores six, it can be classed as therapy and is approved. By contrast, procedure B scores four, and so falls into the enhancement category and is rejected. As wonderful as this may sound, it is not how human beings function; neither is it the way in which God deals with us in his grace.

It is salutary to remind ourselves of a statement about the stature of human beings, which appears in both the Old and New Testaments:

> What are human beings that you are mindful of them, mortals that you care for them? Yet you have made them a little lower than God, and crowned them with glory and honour. You have given them dominion over the works of your hands; you have put all things under their feet ... (Psalm 8:4–6)

> What are human beings that you are mindful of them, or mortals, that you care for them? You have made them for a little

while lower than the angels; you have crowned them with glory
and honour, subjecting all things under their feet.

Now in subjecting all things to them, God left nothing outside their control. As it is, we do not yet see everything in sub-
jection to them, but we do see Jesus ... (Hebrews 2:6–9)

It is interesting reading these words against a backdrop of the
frequently expressed criticism that scientists overreach themselves and act as if they were gods, masters of their fate and of
the destiny of all around them. Biomedical scientists repeatedly come in for this condemnation; they are sinners, who
need to step back and change their attitudes and expectations.
Nothing less will save the world from a future bearing little
resemblance to the present, a future without hope, a future as
bleak as if there had been a nuclear holocaust.

And yet the biblical writers who penned these words did
not appear to think in exactly these terms. For them, the
grandeur of the human condition could not be ignored, even
while acknowledging that much had gone wrong, that human
beings had lost their way, and that they needed direction.
While these words taken in isolation do not pretend to provide a complete theology of the human situation, they remind
us of crucial juxtapositions: our elevated stature alongside our
mortality, our authority over the creation together with our
own need to be subject to a higher authority, the way in which
we are cared for by God over against the care and control we
are to exercise over the creation and others in the human
community.

It is in the working-out of these juxtapositions that we
live truly human existences, powerful and yet humble, leaders
and yet willing to be led, making use of potentially transformative technologies but accepting their limitations and our
own proclivity to misuse them and be led astray by them. We

should not shun the possibilities inherent in being designers of the future, but the balance between being sinners and saints requires immense wisdom, discernment and understanding, all of which are enhanced by a living relationship with the God who cares for us and who experienced human existence in the person of Jesus Christ.

Questions for group discussion

Chapter 1: Should We be Meddling in God's World?

1. What is your understanding of the term "playing God"? Is it a completely negative one, or do you think it may have some positive aspects to it?

2. Consider the six illustrations. What do you see as the major differences between the actions of the couples in 1 and 6, and between the couples in 2 and 3? How do you respond to the couple in illustration 5?

3. Think about the couple with cystic fibrosis in their family. How would you act in a similar situation? If you could afford it, would you go down the path of using pre-implantation genetic diagnosis (PGD)?

4. How much do you think we should use technology in medicine? Do you think it shows a lack of faith in God to use high-technology medicine? Should we expect God to heal all our illnesses without resorting to scientific medicine?

5. Very often, human life is described as being sacred. Does this mean that all life, including that of embryos and fetuses, has absolute value? And if it does, what might this mean? Do we routinely act as if it does, for example, in wars? Did Jesus regard his own life as having absolute value?

Chapter 2: Designer Babies: Who is the Designer?

1. Do you think we routinely attempt to design our children in any way, even when no technological assistance is involved?

2. Why do you think so many people are worried about the possibilities opened up by genetics? Do we exaggerate its power, or is it simply that its power is immense? How do you think its power compares with that of something like nuclear energy?

3. Do you think there is a place for any manipulation of embryos, even for very good purposes? What Christian principles are you using in reaching a conclusion?

4. Imagine you know that a family history of breast cancer is genetic in origin and that this gene can be detected and eliminated in embryos. Would you consider making use of this test via IVF and PGD (putting aside issues of cost)? What issues would you have to consider in arriving at a decision?

5. The role of humility has been emphasised as a helpful Christian virtue in assessing how best to approach the design issues raised by genetics. Do you agree with this, and are there any other virtues you think should be stressed?

Chapter 3: What is Special About the Human Embryo?

1. Why do you think that, for numerous Christians, conception is regarded as the beginning of meaningful (purposeful) human life? Do you think this position has a clear biblical basis?

2. When you think about the beginning of individual human life, how much value do you ascribe to it? Do you think a very early embryo has the same value as yourself? If not, what value does it have? Are these important questions?

3. Regardless of what your own position on the moral status of the human embryo may be, do you think pluralist societies should approve of research on human embryos prior to fourteen days' gestation?

4. Do you think it is possible to value everyone equally? Do we do this in practice? Against this background, do we value all embryos (and fetuses) equally?

5. What are the most important points to emerge from the biblical writers on the value of human life, including life before birth? Distinguish between certainties and uncertainties.

Chapter 4: The Enigma and Challenge of Stem Cells

1. Do you think it is possible to map out in advance ethical and theological principles to govern scientific work that has not yet been undertaken? Think of the discussion on cloning in the 1960s and 1970s.

2. Do you think that the use of ASCs would solve all the ethical problems that might arise with the use of stem cells for research and therapy?

3. Should we ban the use of ESCs if we consider that they raise moral problems, even though they might prove very beneficial in the alleviation of a wide array of diseases suffered by children and adults?

4. Assess the respective contributions of Hui, Shannon and Walter, and Peters to the debate on the worth of embryos. Are you concerned at the diversity of viewpoints within Christian circles? If so, why?

5. In what way does the Bible help us in thinking about embryos and ESCs? Do you expect it to emerge with definitive guidelines in an area like this one?

Chapter 5: The Human Person: Is Neuroscience a Danger to Our Well-being?

1. What do the cases of people like Gage and Zasetsky tell us about the relationship between our brains and what we are as people?

2. What do you think about the two models of the brain touched on in this chapter – the machine model versus the personal model?

3. How would you respond to the proposition that something (brain tissue or cells, or a computer chip) be implanted into your brain?

4. If your brain could be "improved" in some way, would you make use of it? What issues do you think this would raise for you?

5. How do you think Christians should respond to the close relationship between the functioning of our brains and what we are as people?

6. How much do you use the terms "mind" and "soul"? What do they signify, and how important do you think they are?

Chapter 6: A Possible Future World: Clones and Cyborgs

1. How realistic do you think the 2060 scenario is likely to be? In your view, is it overstating or understating the extent of possible developments?

2. Imagine that the first child to be cloned has just been born. What headline would you give to an article in a newspaper describing this event?

3. Explain your feelings about the cloning of human beings. To what extent do your feelings stem from Christian principles?

4. Do you think that the Internet and the whole realm of cyberspace are simply useful technological developments, or are they likely to have much more profound repercussions for how we think of ourselves?

5. Are there limits to the extent to which artificial devices should be used in our bodies? If so, which devices are acceptable and which are not acceptable? And why?

6. Does the use of artificial devices in our bodies tell us anything about our trust in God, and about the alleged superiority of the natural over the artificial?

Chapter 7: Repairing and Manipulating People: Medicine Too Far?

1. What manipulatory forces exist within the society in which we live?

2. How far do you think the concept of the image of God takes us in our thinking about the best ways of responding to current medical technologies? Does the idea of stewardship help?

3. The creativity of human beings is evident in numerous spheres of human activity. Why do we tend to see it as a danger in some realms but not in others? Think especially of the genetic and neural realms.

4. Would you prefer to be living in 1900 rather than today? What influences your answer?

5. Do you think we could put a stop to all biomedical developments? Would you advocate a moratorium if it were possible? Why?

6. Would you feel threatened by the prospect of all genetic (or neural) knowledge about you being made available to other people? What would be at stake from a Christian angle?

Chapter 8: Being Human in a Scientific World

1. To what extent do you recognise a conflict between scientific and religious approaches to the use of technologies at the beginning of human life?

2. What do you see as the relationship between science and ethics? Is it true that scientific developments have to occur before ethical and theological analysis can be brought to bear on them?

3. Think about the relationship between God's care and God's control. Can human beings exert too much control over their world? Can they show too much *care* for their world?

4. Do you think the suffering of the infertile is of the same nature as the suffering of the cancer patient? In what sense does God suffer?

5. Do you think the different ways in which this chapter approaches embryos (via sacrifice and innocence) help us in tackling some of the difficult issues surrounding them?

6. Is there any such thing as a Christian approach to embryos? How much diversity of approach do you think is possible within the Christian church?

Glossary

Adult stem cells: stem cells derived from tissues other than the early embryo, such as fetal or adult organs and tissue. Blood and bone marrow are the best-known examples.

Alzheimer's disease (AD): the most common cause of dementia, a neurodegenerative disorder characterised initially by disturbances of memory, and eventually by severe changes in personality.

Amniocentesis: a test in which some of the amniotic fluid surrounding the fetus is withdrawn from the amniotic sac and analysed for abnormal genes or chromosomes; carried out at around 14–18 weeks' gestation. Frequently conducted to test for chromosomal abnormalities such as Down's syndrome.

Amygdala: an almond-shaped group of cells in the temporal lobe of the brain; a major part of the limbic system that controls the emotions, and especially violence.

Aneuploidy: The condition of having an abnormal number of chromosomes. An example is Down's syndrome, where there are three, rather than two, copies of chromosome 21.

Anterior commissure: a fibre bundle running between the two cerebral hemispheres of the brain. Important for maintaining communication between the right and left sides of the brain.

Assisted reproductive technologies (ARTs): medical treatments designed to help couples with fertility problems achieve pregnancy; involves the manipulation of both eggs and sperm; IVF is the best-known example.

Blastocyst: name given to an early embryo at four to five days' gestation after it reaches the cavity of the uterus; consists of a sphere of cells, with a fluid-filled cavity. The cells of the inner cell mass give rise to the future individual; the outer trophectoderm develops into the placenta.

Blastomere: one cell of a blastocyst.

Central nervous system (CNS): a term used to describe the brain and spinal cord.

Cerebral cortex: the layer of grey matter (nerve cells) forming the outer, or visible, part of the cerebral hemispheres of the brain.

Cerebral hemispheres: the largest parts of the brain in humans; control higher functions of thought, memory, language, sensation and voluntary movements.

Cloning: asexual reproduction, in which the nucleus (and chromosomes) of an ovum (egg) is replaced with the nucleus of a somatic (body) cell of an adult. This causes the ovum to develop as if it had been fertilised without the involvement of sperm. There are two types of cloning: therapeutic (research) cloning and reproductive cloning.

Congenital abnormality: a structural or chemical imperfection present at birth.

Cyberspace: term originated by the author William Gibson in his novel *Neuromancer*. The word "Cyberspace" is currently used to describe the whole range of information resources available through computer networks.

Cyborg: a human with one or more mechanical or electronic devices implanted within their body, in order to enhance the capabilities of that person.

Cystic fibrosis: a genetic disorder resulting from a single-gene defect in which the sufferer's lungs, intestines and pancreas become clogged with thick mucus.

Dementia: irreversible and progressive impairment of mental functions; including intellectual deterioration, disordered personality and an inability to carry out the tasks of daily living.

DNA (deoxyribose nucleic acid): a double-stranded, helical molecule found in the nucleus of a cell; carries the genetic information necessary for the organisation and functioning of most living cells and controls the inheritance of characteristics.

Down's syndrome: a genetic disorder characterised by symptoms of severe mental retardation and heart and respiratory defects; results from an extra copy of chromosome 21.

Duchenne's muscular dystrophy: an inherited disorder characterised by rapidly progressing muscle weakness of the legs and pelvis; later affecting the whole body. It appears in early childhood and survival is rare beyond the late twenties.

Egg: the female gamete, also referred to as an oocyte or ovum, from a woman's ovary.

Embryo: the stage of development from fertilisation up to eight weeks' gestation in humans, by which point all the major organs have been laid down. The first two weeks after fertilisation are variously referred to as pre-embryo or pre-implantation embryo.

Embryonic disc: a flat, circular structure formed from the inner cell mass at the same time that implantation of the blastocyst into the uterus occurs. The two layers of the embryonic disc will give rise to all the tissues of the body.

Embryonic stem cells (ESCs): stem cells derived from the inner cell mass of early embryos (blastocysts).

Fertilisation: the act of rendering gametes capable of further development; begins with contact between spermatozoon and ovum, leading to their fusion, which stimulates the completion of ovum maturation.

Fetus (foetus): the developing human being from the end of the eighth week of gestation until birth.

Frontal lobes: the frontal regions of the cerebral hemispheres, which are responsible for higher thought processes.

Functional magnetic resonance imaging (fMRI): a non-invasive procedure that produces two-dimensional images of the flow of blood to functioning areas of the brain.

Gene: a unit of DNA in a chromosome; the biological unit of heredity.

Gene therapy: the replacement of a gene responsible for a disease such as cystic fibrosis by a (normal) gene in an attempt to remove that disease from the individual; this can be carried out in the embryo or in the individual after birth.

Genetic engineering: the manipulation of genetic information in an embryo in order to control the characteristics of the future individual; the term is frequently used in a negative, critical sense.

Genetic enhancement: use of techniques to manipulate the genetic information of an organism in order to improve its characteristics, rather than to correct deficiencies.

Genetic testing: a test to determine whether a person has certain gene changes (mutations) or chromosome changes which are known to cause or increase the risk for certain diseases.

Genome: the entire genetic material of an organism; includes the genetic material located in both the nucleus and the mitochondria.

Gestation: the period of development from the time of fertilisation of the ovum until birth.

Hemophilia: a genetic disease characterised by the absence of an essential clotting factor in the blood; results in excessive bleeding following injury.

Human Leukocyte Antigen tissue-typing (HLA): an additional step to PGD to determine whether an embryo could result in a child who could provide a tissue match for transplantation to an ill sibling.

Hypothalamus: the region of the brain that controls body temperature, thirst, hunger, water balance, and sexual function. It also plays a role in emotional activity and sleep.

Implantation: the embedding of the early embryo (between six and fourteen days' gestation) in the lining of the uterus (womb), so that further development of the embryo can take place.

Inner cell mass (ICM): the cluster of cells in a blastocyst which protrude into the fluid-filled cavity, and subsequently develop into the embryo proper and some of the supporting tissues; four to six days' gestation.

***In vitro* fertilisation (IVF):** the process of fertilising a (human) egg with a (human) sperm *in vitro* in the laboratory and therefore outside the body of the woman. Embryo transfer may follow, and the term "IVF" is used to cover both the fertilisation and the embryo transfer.

Leukemia: a cancer of the blood.

Limbic system: a set of brain structures deep within the brain that generates our feelings, emotions, and motivations. It is also important in learning and memory.

Mitochondria: small structures (organelles) within a cell that are responsible for energy production.

Morula: a solid mass of blastomeres that forms when the zygote splits.

Nephritis: inflammation of the kidneys.

Nerve cells (neurons): one of the major classes of cell in the nervous system. They are the fundamental signalling units of the nervous system and conduct electrical impulses from one part of the body to another.

Neural plate: one of the earliest indications of the nervous system, appearing at around three weeks after fertilisation.

Neural progenitor cells (NPCs): stem cells found in the CNS that are capable of maturing into either neurons or glial cells.

Neural transplantation: the transfer of neural tissue from human fetuses into the brains of patients with neurodegenerative disorders in an attempt to relieve the symptoms of the disease.

Neurotransmitter: a chemical substance released at synapses (for example dopamine, serotonin) and used by neurons to communicate with each other and with other types of cell.

Non-therapeutic research: clinical research which has, as its primary goal, the acquisition of knowledge rather than the benefit of the patient (therapeutic research).

Oocyte: precursor of a woman's egg; often used loosely to refer to the egg.

Ovum: egg.

Parkinson's disease: a progressive neurodegenerative disease characterised by motor disorders, in particular tremor and a general decrease in normal movements.

Persistent vegetative state (PVS): a condition resulting from severe damage to the higher centres of the brain; after a few months most authorities consider the condition to be permanent. The patient is unable to engage in any mental activity but retains the ability to swallow, breathe and blink, and can absorb nutrients supplied through a nasogastric tube.

Person: sometimes used as a synonym for "human being", but increasingly used to mean a sentient being that has a concept of itself, and is capable of reflective, rational thought.

Personhood: the term used to describe that which characterises those who are persons, and who are to be valued and treated as equal to the rest of us.

Placenta: the special tissue that joins the mother to her fetus; it provides the fetus with oxygen, water and nutrients from the mother's blood, eliminates waste, and secretes the hormones necessary for successful pregnancy.

Plasticity: the ability of cells and tissues to be influenced by, and respond to, ongoing activity. A term commonly used in connection with the nervous system.

Pluripotent: the ability of a cell or group of cells to give rise to all of the cell types that constitute an individual, but not the individual as a whole.

Pre-implantation embryo: a name given to the entire product of the fertilised egg up to the end of the implantation stage (fourteen days). Also referred to as the pre-embryo.

Pre-implantation genetic diagnosis (PGD): a procedure devised to test early human embryos for serious inherited genetic conditions, with the subsequent transfer of only unaffected embryos to a woman's uterus.

Primitive streak: a thickening of the ectoderm which appears in the human embryo at fourteen to fifteen days' gestation. Often considered to represent the transition from a non-organised to an organised state during embryonic development. Its appearance marks the end of the time during which research can be undertaken on embryos.

Regeneration: the process whereby lost or injured cells, tissues or organs are able to regrow.

Reproductive cloning: the use of somatic-cell nuclear transfer (SCNT) to produce genetically identical human beings.

Serotonin: a chemical that functions as a neurotransmitter, and has many effects, including blood vessel constriction and smooth muscle stimulation.

Sex-linked disorder: a disorder caused by a mutation to a gene carried on a sex chromosome (X or Y). For example, hemophilia is the result of a gene defect on the X chromosome.

Somatic-cell nuclear transfer (SCNT): the transfer of the nucleus of a somatic (body) cell of an adult into an ovum which has had its nucleus removed; also known as cloning.

Somatic cells: the ordinary cells in an organism (that is, not the reproductive cells).

Stem cells: undifferentiated cells which can divide indefinitely, and in some cases are capable of forming any cell type in the body.

Striatum: an area of the brain intimately involved in the control of movement.

Surrogacy: one woman bearing a child for another woman, where the surrogate carries the embryo of the commissioning parents, or is artificially inseminated with sperm from the partner of the second woman. It may involve IVF.

Synaptic connection (synapse): the physiological connection between nerve cells, across which they communicate with each other by using chemicals called neurotransmitters.

Tay Sachs disease: a genetic disorder resulting from a single-gene defect in which lipids accumulate in the nervous tissue, resulting in death in early childhood.

Temporal lobes: the lateral regions of the cerebral hemispheres, which are responsible for a range of functions, including hearing and the recognition of objects.

Therapeutic (research) cloning: the use of SCNT to produce tissues for medical purposes rather than complete human beings.

Therapeutic research: a scientific project which has the aim of directly benefiting the person on whom the research is being conducted.

Totipotent: referring to the ability of a cell or group of cells to give rise to a complete individual.

Trophoblast: the membrane that forms the wall of the blastocyst in early development, and aids implantation in the uterine wall. After implantation the trophoblast divides into two layers, one of which is the placenta.

Trophoectoderm: the outer cell layer of the blastocyst, and the precursor of the placenta.

Turner's syndrome: a chromosome abnormality affecting only females, caused by the complete or partial deletion of the X chromosome, characterised by short stature and non-functioning ovaries.

Uterus: hollow muscular organ in the female body, in which the fertilised ovum normally becomes embedded, and in which the developing embryo and fetus is nourished.

Zygote: the product of the union of the male and female gametes at fertilisation; a fertilised egg.

Bibliography

Alexander, Denis and White, Robert. *Beyond Belief*. Lion Publishing, Oxford, 2004.

Allen, L.S. and Gorski, R.A. "Sexual orientation and the size of the anterior commissure in the human brain." *Proceedings of the National Academy of Sciences* 1992, 89, 7199–7202.

Arnst, Catherine. "I can't remember." *Business Week* 1 September 2003. http://www.businessweek.com

Atkinson, Robert D. "Some theological perspectives on the human embryo." In Nigel M. de S. Cameron (ed.) *Embryos and Ethics: The Warnock Report in Debate*. Rutherford House Books, Edinburgh, 1987, pp. 43–57.

Barth, Karl. *Church Dogmatics*. Volume III/4, G.W. Bromiley and T.F. Torrance (eds), T. and T. Clark, Edinburgh, 1961.

Board for Social Responsibility of the Church of England. *Cybernauts Awake!* Church House Publishing, London, 1999.

Bouma, Hessell, Diekema, Douglas, Langerak, Edward, Rottman, Theodore and Verhey, Allen. *Christian Faith, Health and Medical Practice*. Eerdmans, Grand Rapids, 1989, pp. 4–5.

Bryant, John and Searle, John. *Life in our Hands: A Christian Perspective on Genetics and Cloning*. Inter-Varsity Press, Leicester, 2004.

Cameron, Nigel M. de S. "The Christian stake in the Warnock

debate." In Nigel M. de S. Cameron (ed.), *Embryos and Ethics*. Rutherford House Books, Edinburgh, 1987, pp. 1–13.

Caplan, Arthur. "Open your mind." *The Economist*, 23 May 2002, 73–75.

Clough, David. *Unweaving the Web*. Grove Books, Cambridge, 2002.

Cochrane Menstrual Disorders and Subfertility Group for the New Zealand Guidelines Group. *Systematic Review of the Quantifiable Harms and Benefits of Preimplantation Genetic Diagnosis*. Advice for the National Ethics Committee on Assisted Human Reproduction and the Ministry of Health, 2004.

Cole-Turner, Ronald. *The New Genesis: Theology and the Genetic Revolution*. Westminster, John Knox Press, Louisville, 1993.

Committee on the Biological and Biomedical Applications of Stem Cell Research. *Stem Cells and the Future of Regenerative Medicine*. National Academy Press, Washington DC, 2002.

Cook, Gareth. "New technique eyed in stem-cell debate." *The Boston Globe*, November 21, 2004.

Dutney, Andrew. *Playing God: Ethics and Faith*. HarperCollins Religious, Melbourne, 2001.

Eisenberg, Leon. "Would cloned humans really be like sheep?" *New England Journal of Medicine* 1999, 340:6, 471–475.

Ellul, Jacques. *The Technological Society*. John Wilkinson (translator), Jonathan Cape, London, 1964.

ESHRE PGD Consortium Steering Committee. "ESHRE preimplantation genetic diagnosis consortium: Data collection III (May 2001)". *Human Reproduction* 2002, 17, 233–246.

Ezzell, Carol. "Why? The neuroscience of suicide." *Scientific American*, February 2003, 44–51.

Farah, Martha J. and Wolpe, Paul Root. "Monitoring and manipulating brain function: New neuroscience technologies and their ethical implications." *Hastings Center Report* 2004, 34, 35–45.

Fletcher, Joseph. *The Ethics of Genetic Control*. Anchor Books, Garden City, New York, 1974.

Ford, Norman. *When Did I Begin?* Cambridge University Press, Cambridge, 1988.

Hefner, Philip. "The evolution of the created co-creator." In Ted Peters (ed.) *Cosmos as Creation: Science and Theology in Consonance*. Abingdon Press, Nashville, 1989, pp. 211–233.

Hui, Edwin C. *At the Beginning of Life: Dilemmas in Theological Bioethics*. InterVarsity Press, Downers Grove, Illinois, 2002.

Human Genetics Commission. *Choosing the Future: Genetics and Reproductive Decision Making*. Department of Health, London, 2004.

Iglesias, Teresa. "What kind of being is the human embryo?" In Nigel M. de S. Cameron (ed.) *Embryos and Ethics*. Rutherford House Books, Edinburgh, 1987, pp. 58–73.

Jeeves, Malcolm. "How free is free? Reflections on the neuropsychology of thought and action." *Science and Christian Belief* 2003, 16, 101–122.

Jonas, Hans. *Philosophical Essays: From Ancient Creed to Technological Man*. Prentice-Hall, Englewood Cliffs, New Jersey, 1974.

Jones, D. Gareth. *Manufacturing Humans*, Inter-Varsity Press, Leicester, 1987.

Jones, D. Gareth. "Fetal neural transplantation: Placing the ethical debate within the context of society's use of human material." *Bioethics* 1991, 5, 23–42.

Jones, D. Gareth. "The human embryo: Between oblivion and meaningful life." *Science and Christian Belief* 1994, 6, 3–19.

Jones, D. Gareth. "The problematic symmetry between brain

birth and brain death." *Journal of Medical Ethics* 1998, 24, 237–242.

Jones, D. Gareth. *Valuing People*. Paternoster, Carlisle, 1999.

Jones, D. Gareth. "The human embryo: A reassessment of theological approaches in the light of scientific developments." *Stimulus* 2000a, 8, 38–45.

Jones, D. Gareth. *Speaking for the Dead. Cadavers in Biology and Medicine*. Ashgate Publishers, Aldershot, 2000b.

Jones, D. Gareth. *Clones: The Clowns of Technology?* Paternoster, Carlisle, 2001.

Jones, D. Gareth. "Biomedical manipulation: Arguing the case for a cautiously optimistic stance." *Perspectives on Science and Christian Faith* 2002a, 54, 93–102.

Jones, D. Gareth. "Human cloning: A watershed for science and ethics?" *Science and Christian Belief* 2002b, 14, 159–180.

Jones, D. Gareth. "A neurobiological portrait of the human person: Finding a context for approaching the brain." In Joel B. Green (ed.), *What about the Soul? Neuroscience and Christian Anthropology*. Abingdon Press, Nashville, 2004a, pp. 31–46.

Jones, D. Gareth. "Embryos and people: The perplexity of our beginnings." *Stimulus* 2004b, 14, 20–26.

Jones, D. Gareth. "Responses to the human embryo and embryonic stem cells: Scientific and theological assessments." *Science and Christian Belief* 2005, in press.

Jones, D. Gareth and Galvin, Kerry. "Neural grafting in Parkinson's disease: Scientific and ethical pitfalls on the road from basic science to clinical reality." *Research Communications in Biological Psychology and Psychiatry*, 2005, in press.

Jones, D. Gareth and Sagee, Sharon. "Xenotransplantation: Hope or delusion?" *Biologist* 2001, 48, 129–132.

Jones, Nancy L. and Kilner, John F. *Genetics, Biotechnology and the Future*. The Center for Bioethics and Human Dignity, April 8 2004. http://cbhd.org/resources/genetics/jones_kilner_2004-04-08.htm

Kahn, Axel. "Clone mammals ... Clone man?" *Nature* 1997, 386, 119.

Kass, Leon. "The wisdom of repugnance." In Gregory Pence (ed.), *Flesh of My Flesh: The Ethics of Cloning Humans*. Rowman and Littlefield, Lanham, MD, 1998, pp. 13–37.

Kolata, Gina. *Clone: The Road to Dolly, and the Path Ahead*. Penguin Books, London, 1998.

Le Vay, Simon. "A difference in hypothalamic structure between heterosexual and homosexual men." *Science* 1991, 253, 1034–1037.

Levitt, Pat, Reinoso, B., Jones, L. "The critical impact of early cellular environment on neuronal development." *Preventive Medicine* 1998, 27, 180–183.

Krauthammer, Charles *et al.* "A special report on cloning." *Time*, 10 March 1997, 40–53.

Luria, Alexander R. *The Man with a Shattered World* (L. Solotaroff, trans.). Penguin Books, Harmondsworth, 1975.

Lutzer, Erwin. "*Biotechnology's brave new world*." The Center for Bioethics and Human Dignity, November 21, 2003. http://cbhd.org/resources/biotech/lutzer_2003-11-21.htm

McCarthy, B. *Fertility and Faith*. Inter-Varsity Press, Leicester, 1997, p. 75.

McCormick, Richard A. *How Brave a New World?* SCM Press, London, 1981.

MacKay, Donald M. *Human Science and Human Dignity*. Hodder and Stoughton, London, 1979.

MacKay, Donald M. "The beginnings of personal life." *In the Service of Medicine* 1984, 30, 9–13.

MacKay, Donald M. "The ethics of brain manipulation." In

Richard L. Gregory (ed.), *The Oxford Companion to the Mind*. Oxford University Press, Oxford, 1987a, pp. 113–114.

MacKay, Donald M. "Brain science and the soul." In Richard L. Gregory (ed.), *The Oxford Companion to the Mind*. Oxford University Press, Oxford, 1987b, pp. 723–725.

MacKay, Donald M. *The Open Mind and Other Essays: A scientist in God's world*. Inter-Varsity Press, Leicester, 1988, pp. 54–65.

Maguire, G. and McGee, Ellen. "Implantable brain chips? Time for debate." *Hastings Center Report* 1999, 29, 7–13.

Meilaender, Gilbert. *Bioethics*. Eerdmans, Grand Rapids, 1996.

Meilaender, Gilbert. "Begetting and cloning." In Gregory Pence (ed.), *Flesh of My Flesh: The Ethics of Cloning Humans*. Rowman and Littlefield, Lanham, MD, 1998, pp. 39–44.

Meilaender, Gilbert. "The point of a ban. Or, how to think about stem cell research." *Hastings Center Report* 2001, 31, 9–16.

Meyer, J.R. "Human embryonic stem cells and respect for life." *Journal of Medical Ethics* 2000, 26, 166–170.

Mussa-Ivaldi, Ferdinando A. and Miller, Lee E. "Brain-machine interfaces: Computational demands and clinical needs meet basic neuroscience." *Trends in Neurosciences* 2003, 26, 329–334.

National Institutes of Health. *Stem cells: Scientific progress and future research directions*. Department of Health and Human Services, June 2001. http://stemcell.nih.gov/info/scireport/.

Nelson, Lawrence J. "Preimplantation diagnosis." *Clinics in Perinatology* 2003, 30, 67–80.

Nuffield Council on Bioethics. *Genetics and Behaviour: The Ethical Context*. Nuffield Council on Bioethics, London, 2002.

O'Donovan, Oliver. *Begotten or Made?* Clarendon Press, Oxford, 1984.

Parker, Malcolm, Forbes, Kevin and Findlay, Ian. "Eugenics or empowered choice? Community issues arising from pre-natal testing." *Australian and New Zealand Journal of Obstetrics and Gynecology* 2002, 42, 10–14.

Pellegrino, Edmund D. *"Biotechnology, human enhancement, and the ends of medicine."* The Center for Bioethics and Human Dignity, November 30, 2004.

Peters, Ted. *Playing God? Genetic Determinism and Human Freedom.* Routledge, New York, 2003a.

Peters, Ted. "Embryonic persons in the cloning and stem cell debates." *Theology and Science* 2003b, 1, 51–77.

Peterson, James C. *Genetic Turning Points.* Eerdmans, Grand Rapids, 2001.

Ramsey, Paul. *Fabricated Man.* Yale University Press, New Haven, 1970, p. 151.

Sandel, Michael J. "The case against perfection." *The Atlantic Monthly*, April 2004, 293, pp. 51–62.

Shannon, Thomas A. and Walter, James J. *The New Genetic Medicine.* Rowman and Littlefield, Lanham, Maryland, 2003.

Stassen, Glen and Gushee, David. *Kingdom Ethics.* InterVarsity Press, Downers Grove, Illinois, 2003, pp. 222–223.

Swerdlow, Russell and Burns, Jeffrey. "Right orbitofrontal tumor with pedophilia symptom and constructional apraxia sign." *Archives of Neurology* 2003, 60, 437–440.

Tardoff, Kenneth. "Unusual diagnoses among violent patients." *The Psychiatric Clinics of North America* 1998, 21, 576–576.

The Christian Institute. *Demolishing Arguments.* The Christian Institute, Newcastle upon Tyne, 2003.

Towns, Cindy. *Embryonic Stem Cell Research: Understanding and Analysis at the Interfaces of Science, Medicine and Ethics.* PhD thesis, University of Otago, 2004.

Towns, Cindy R. and Jones, D. Gareth. "Stem cells, embryos, and the environment: A context for both science and ethics." *Journal of Medical Ethics* 2004a, 30, 410–413.

Towns, Cindy R. and Jones, D. Gareth. "Stem cells: Science, ethics and public policy." *New Zealand Bioethics Journal* 2004b, 5, 22–28.

Valenstein, Elliot S. *Brain Control*. John Wiley and Sons, New York, 1973.

Walzer, Michael. *Just and Unjust Wars: A Moral Argument with Historical Illustrations*. Basic Books, New York, 1977.

Watt, Fiona and Hogan, Brigid. "Out of Eden: Stem cells and their niches." *Science* 2000, 287, 1427–1430.

Index

Index of Names

Index of
Scriptural References

255

Printed and bound by CPI Group (UK) Ltd, Croydon, CR0 4YY

13/04/2025

14656477-0001